"It is almost unbearable to go through some of life's challenges, wondering how God will allow a certain tragedy into our lives. Be inspired by the Lord's unveiling of his perfect plan through life and death. In this case, we've personally seen the blessing."

Albert & Deidre Pujols
St. Louis Cardinals

"In ways beyond the explanations of reason, when pain meets faith—faith can grow. When tragedy took his beloved, Jason Mirikitani struggled with loss, grief, loneliness, anger and what to believe. His journey past the tragedy at Mile Marker 825 led him through each and into the joys of a faith that first comforted, then strengthened and, finally, renewed. Mile Marker 825 is about terrible heartbreak and life-giving hope."

Dr. Bryan Chapell
President
Covenant Theological Seminary

"Even though I knew Jason's story before I read this wonderful book I was moved to tears of both joy and sorrow as I turned its pages. Jason presents the tragedy of his accident and the remarkable account of his recovery in a way that will grip your heart and mind. He neither diminishes the sadness, nor fails to be amazed by the kindness and power of God in recounting the drama of his life. He sets his personal story in the context of the greater story of our human brokenness and of God's redeeming love in a manner that makes compelling reading. Buy this book for yourself. Get more copies to give to your friends."

Jerram Barrs
Professor of Systematic Theology
Covenant Theological Seminary

"Few people have gone through the pain and heartbreak that Jason has gone through. I never cease to be amazed at the incredible grace that is found within the tears and restoration of the miracle of Jason's life. If you need hope, then listen to this story; you will definitely find it."

Joel Engle
Pastor, The Exchange Church
Keller, Texas
Musician, www.joelengle.com

And we know that God causes all things to work together for good to those who love God, to those who are called according to His purpose.

Romans 8:28

"Can tragedy be synonymous with blessing? Can water that brings life be found in a desert? A story of great faith and unexplainable perseverance lies within these pages. I pray that your heart may be encouraged as it is taken on this journey, a journey of great loss; great loss met by an even greater faith in God, a Savior who in His sovereignty can and will bring life from the ashes."

Shane Everett
Musician, Shane & Shane
www.shaneandshane.com

"Peter likened tested faith to gold refined by fire. Jason Mirikitani's faith has been refined by suffering, and now through smoke and flame he testifies. Praise be to the mighty God who sustained him in all his woe, and praise God we get to read the story."

Dr. Jim Hamilton
Associate Professor of Biblical Theology
The Southern Baptist Theological Seminary

"Mile Marker 825 will grip you and keep you reading. Every time I see or talk with Jason Mirikitani I am reminded by his story and his life that God is a faithful covenant keeping God. If you are wondering how God's grace can overflow in your life through the most difficult circumstances imaginable, I encourage you to read Jason's story."

Dr. Andy Chambers,
Vice President for Student Development,
Professor of Bible,
Missouri Baptist University, St. Louis, MO

"In your hands, you have an inspiring, challenging and honest story by a man who has lived out one of the biggest fears we all face. This is a story of death and pain, of hope and healing... Jason shares this story because so many of us are dealing with the same issues of death, loss and pain. If you haven't already, many of you will face these issues soon—it's not a matter of if, but a matter of when. It is Jason's wish that, when the time comes, you will rebuild your life with the same hope and healing that drives the answer to the question, 'What are you going to do now?'"

Dr. Joe White
President, Kanakuk Kamps

"I want to compare faith to running in a race. It's hard. It requires concentration of will, energy of soul. You experience elation when the winner breaks the tape—especially if you've got a bet on it. But how long does that last? You go home. Maybe your dinner's burnt. Maybe you haven't got a job. So who am I to say, 'Believe, have faith,' in the face of life's realities? I would like to give you something more permanent, but I can only point the way. I have no formula for winning the race. Everyone runs in her own way, or his own way. And where does the power come from, to see the race to its end? From within."

—Eric Liddell, *Chariots of Fire* (1981)[1]

---

1   *Chariots of Fire.* Twentieth Century Fox Film Company, 1981.

Mile Marker
825

A Widower's Survival &
Resurrected Hope

Mile Marker
825

A Widower's Survival &
Resurrected Hope

JASON D. MIRIKITANI

LUCIDBOOKS

MILE MARKER 825

ACKNOWLEDGMENTS

I am grateful to countless people who helped save and restore my life; most notably my mom, dad, and brother, in addition to Sergeant Troy Dick, the hospital staff at Christus St. Elizabeth Hospital in Beaumont, TX, and other close friends. I am richly blessed that I could almost compose a small book with a list of all the people who helped me in my recovery. I mention some of them specifically in Chapter 6. But I will use this space to acknowledge those who have contributed to my writing the book in your hands.

Thank you faculty of Covenant Theological Seminary, led by Dr. Bryan Chapell, a man that many would say has countless reasons to be arrogant but instead walks in genuine humility. Whenever I would see him on campus, he'd always shake my hand and address me personally: "Hi, Jason." I thank Covenant because I now realize that the living God led me to this institution and to professors like Jerram Barrs who would personify God's *grace* to me and teach His grace to me clearly, even though this grace seemed uncertain or unavailable to me for a dreadful season of my life. I am thrilled that my theological studies happened at Covenant, genuinely rooting me in God's grace.

Thank you, Jon Lux, my initial editor. Since you were already my buddy, I knew you'd shoot me straight. I thought you were cool at Shiloh. I just had no idea you were so smart too.

Thank you Kelli Stuart for being a brilliant copy editor who could make twists, turns, and adjustments to my writing that would ultimately transform it into an appealing book.

You are excellent at what you do. I am thrilled that you are the wife of my good friend.

And on a personal note, I am grateful to my sweet bride, Christe, who has embraced and encouraged the writing of this book, knowing that its content would bless and offer hope to many. This is especially noteworthy, given its sensitive nature, which a recent conversation illustrates:

I mentioned the book to the youth Sunday school class at church one week, and a 14 year old looked at me and asked, "Isn't this difficult for your wife, Christe, that you've written a book about the car accident that killed your first wife?"

In this matter, Christe has shown such grace herself, strength of character, and commitment to me and to the things of our God. I feel about Christe like Paul felt about the Philippians, "Every time I think of you, I give thanks to my God" (Phil. 1:3, NLT).

Lastly and most importantly, in the writing of this book, specifically in the story that this book describes, and in daily life, I acknowledge my God and His Son Jesus, my Lord and Savior. I personally know that "The LORD is good, a strong refuge when trouble comes. He is close to those who trust in Him" (Nahum 1:7, NLT). I gladly rest in the One who knows me well personally, who even watches out for sparrows, and is certainly watching over me (Matthew 10:29-30). There are many things about Him that I don't understand, but I do know that He loves me more than I can imagine. That's enough for me.

To visit Jason's ministry homepage or read his Blogs, go to www.ourRescuer.com.

DEDICATION

T his book is dedicated to Jill Shirley Mirikitani herself, who has passed the "pearly gates" on into glory already, who was an extremely talented singer on earth, and who now sings directly in the presence of the living God Himself. Although she is no longer with us on earth, I think that she might occasionally peek past the "great cloud of witnesses" (Hebrews 12:1). I hope that she is honored, as I pray that the Lord Himself is honored in this piece as well.

It is also dedicated to her parents, Jakie and Dottie Shirley, and to her brother, Jon Shirley. Thankfully and because of the grace they extend to me, I will always call them my in-laws, and Jakie and Dottie will forever be our children's grandparents in the great state of Texas! How I love, respect, and appreciate these godly people; Jakie and Jon were actually both in the car wreck that this book discusses, but suffered less severe injuries, *physically* that is.

And this work is also dedicated to Sean Glanvill, his siblings, and his unbelievable parents. At age 12, this boy endured a tragic car accident, very similar to mine, in May 2007, and his family members are dear friends of my wife and me. We regularly pray for Sean, believing that the living God will continue a restoring work in his young life.

Generally, I dedicate this book to everyone who endures hardship, trial, or tribulation. I pray that you will personally know the "ever-present help in trouble," the One who readily "lifts us out of muck and mire, and sets our feet on rock, making our steps secure." (Psalm 46:1, 40:2) What a tremendous Rescuer, Restorer, and Refresher He is.

The Shirley family with Abby, Jill, & Jason—Spring 2001

FOREWORD

I n your hands, you have an inspiring, challenging and honest story by a man who has lived out one of the biggest fears we all face.

This is a story of death and pain, of hope and healing.

These are elements to life that will change the very core of a person's soul. They can transform a person into a completely new being. In fact, this is quite often the case. The result is change. Not just simple change that is quickly adjusted to but earth-shattering, bone-crunching, life-altering change.

Change is what most people fear when they think of death and pain. We find ourselves in the seemingly unending cycle of asking ourselves, "What am I going to do now?" It is through hope and healing that we find our answers.

I have known Jason Mirikitani for almost 20 years. He has a heart of gold. His life was changed forever at our sports camps in Missouri. He found his source of hope and healing there long before the tragedy that took the life of his bride, Jill.

After Jason grieved the loss of Jill, after countless hours of physical and emotional rehabilitation, Jason came to the crossroads of "What am I going to do now? Will death and pain be the building blocks of my new life? Or do I build on the hope and healing I have received?"

This book is the answer. Jason heard a still, small, quiet voice that said, "Other people are hurting like you are. Other people are dealing with the same pain you are. Other people need to hear a survival story that will inspire them to create their own."

Jason shares this story because so many of us are dealing with the same issues of death, loss and pain. If you haven't already, many of you will face these issues soon—it's not a matter of if, but a matter of when. It is Jason's wish that, when the time comes, you will rebuild your life with the same hope and healing that drives the answer to the question,

"What are you going to do now?"

Dr. Joe White
President, Kanakuk Kamps

PREFACE

Mile Marker Meaning

As I was considering different title choices for this book, my close friend Sean suggested, "Mile Marker _____," asking if I knew the exact location of the dramatic car accident. He indicated that this title would have a sharp double meaning.

"Milestone," another word for "Mile Marker," is defined in two ways:

1. *A stone marker set up on a roadside to indicate the distance in miles from a given point.*
2. *An important event, as in a person's career, the history of a nation, or the advancement of knowledge in a field; a turning point.*[2]

While this horrific car wreck happened at a specific mile marker near Beaumont, Texas (825), it also marks a significant mile marker in my personal spiritual life, a time of painful but rapid growth as I personally learned that when our God may *seem* most absent and distant, He is actually most present and

---

2   www.thefreedictionary.com

nearby (Psalm 46:1). At this time, "His sufficient grace and power perfected in weakness" (2 Corinthians 12:9) became my daily necessities.

While I would have never asked for what occurred on that January day at Mile Marker 825 on Highway 10, I am forever grateful for the thread of mile markers in my life that began out of it.

Mile Marker 825 on I-10
between Houston and Beaumont, TX

Falling...

Jill, Abby, & Jason in March 2001

January 2002

"Falling in love is not an extension of one's limits or boundaries; it is partial and temporary collapse of them."
—M. Scott Peck

"I've fallen, and I can't get up!"
—LifeCall©

I should preface this chapter by admitting that, in the process of writing this book, I honestly wrote at least three other chapters and several other chapter outlines first. The reason for my delay on this one is not that I'm a procrastinator; it's simply that re-thinking and re-feeling the contents of these first pages has been extremely painful to my heart, sort of like re-opening a healed wound. So I've dreaded doing it, but since you need to know the whole story, here it is.

MILE

On January 15, 2002, 3½ years of happy marriage came to a screeching halt when our car, after five times flipping, crossed a median, and slammed into a tractor-trailer truck. My wife, Jill, died instantly.

And I have never been the same.

I loved Jill so very much. She was my dream girl. I waited 27 years for exactly the right girl to marry—a girl just like Jill. Though originally from St. Louis, I was living at the time in Dallas and working as a youth minister. I had brought in a Christian band to do a concert for our youth group one spring evening. Little did I know that their lead singer had an older sister who lived in Dallas, who would want to come to this concert and support her brother, who would end up warming up to me a bit, who loved the Lord, and who was very pretty. I couldn't have asked for a more perfect set-up.

The evening we met, Jill and I struck up a conversation, and I remember hoping that my pounding heart in my chest was not visible through my shirt! I mean, I was both nervous and excited, to the degree that I felt like a teenager ten years earlier who had first seen an attractive, compelling young lady. She had big blue eyes, beautiful smile, and... she just captivated me! I wanted to learn as much as I could about her. So I asked a lot of questions.

I learned that Jill actually had a master's degree in vocal performance, and taught voice at a local Baptist university. Since I led worship at our youth meetings and sang while playing the guitar (more importantly, because I wanted to make sure I didn't fumble away the opportunity to see this sweet, attractive girl again), I asked her if she wouldn't mind giving me "voice lessons" for a reasonable fee. Thankfully, she agreed, informing me that it would be free (to support our ministry, she said). She then handed me her phone number on a small slip of paper. It occurred to me at that moment that I got a girl's phone number in one of the coolest ways ever. I now realize that she must have also had *some* mutual interest. Looking back I see evidence of God's hand as well. And so that night, my relationship with Jill Shirley began.

I did, of course, anxiously make that important phone call immediately the next morning, and shortly after, my weekly voice lessons began. I learned how to "match pitch" for the first time in my life, a principle I'd never even heard of before. Moreover, Jill taught me some guitar theory, which would truly benefit me in my ability as a worship leader. But while that was all fun and interesting, what I enjoyed more than anything was spending time with my pretty new teacher.

After a handful of lessons, I decided to do something that was beyond *terrifying*—I was going to ask Jill out. I still remember my pulse-rate quickening and my palms sweating. Here I was, 27 years old, yet I felt like a junior high boy trying to get the guts to ask a girl to a Friday night "sock-hop." I dialed her office phone number and then hung up before it started to ring. I did that twice. Finally, after many deep breaths, I let it ring, and Jill answered. I believe I said something like, "Hi… Uh, Jill. This is Jason Mirikitani. Hi. Well, I don't mean to overstep my bounds as your student, but I was wondering if you might wanna have dinner with me, like at a restaurant, one night this weekend." And then there was a pause. "Oh no," I thought, "I really blew it because I sounded too dorky." After what seemed like an eternity, she finally replied, "Sorry about that; I just had to step outside of my office for a second because I had another student in there… but sure, I'd love to go. What kind of food do you like?"

Upon hanging up, I heaved a sigh of relief, then I commenced to dancing and singing (on pitch, of course) around the house. That weekend, Jill and I went on our first official date and began to regularly spend time together, outside of our voice lessons, learning more about one another, our likes and dislikes, our backgrounds, our interests, and our concerns. We laughed together, went on walks together, and grew to understand one another, all in the process of falling in love beyond the initial, mutual attraction.

And what a fun process this was! I learned that Jill was adventurous and proper, mischievous and mannerly, silly and serious. In countless ways, she kept me guessing, and I was doing my best to take mental notes as I was getting to know her better. Regardless, I was just enjoying being with her and laughing together. Whether we were grabbing a late dinner, catching a movie, or doing something extra fun like the high-flying "Sky Coaster" carnival ride (where she sang opera the whole time, something she did whenever she was afraid), our times were always a blast.

By the spring of 1998, I had asked for and received her parents' blessing and set a plan to propose marriage. I thought it would be extra fun and romantic to do a scavenger hunt to many of the sites of our various dates, with rhyming clues stuck to benches and signs at the different locations we enjoyed together. The final clue led her to a shovel and, actually, to the buried engagement ring, which was right next to a small creek and a bridge, which were adjacent to a large stone teddy bear statue. It was the perfect sight for the finale of my romantic mystery maze! By the time she dug up the diamond, I was already on my knee and ready to ask for her hand in marriage. When Jill said, "Yes" to my proposal, I was indeed a joyous man!

We got married that fall on September 26th, 1998. It was magical and special for everyone. Folks who were there still talk about our wedding today, because the ceremony twisted heartstrings, while containing a wide variety of different components, all of which clung to similar themes. For example, it began with a "liturgical dance," a Christian expression of prayer or worship through body movement, to a song comparing God's love for His people to man's love for a woman. The fact that we performed a dance may not sound like a big deal, until one considers that we were wed in a Southern Baptist church. Given the traditions of this particular denomination, allowance of any sort of *dancing* was remarkable, let alone embraced by the pastor marrying us, whose eyes watered during the dance because the performance so touched his heart.

As the ushers escorted guests to their seats, and the groomsmen entered during the wedding processional, my years of working at an inner-city youth camp with numerous African American friends became evident, as a mixture of races filled my side of the sanctuary. What followed was a fairly traditional wedding ceremony, full of both smiles and tears, but people most often recall the conclusion of that sincere nuptial occasion.

As our pastor began to say, "By the power vested in me, it is with great joy..." which would lead to, "I now pronounce you, man and wife. You may kiss your bride." We arranged for the classical music (performed by the London Symphony Orchestra) from "Superman—The Movie" to begin playing over the church sound system. Since childhood, I have been a Superman fan, something that many of my friends know about me. What was especially comical about this particular happening was that not everyone was certain as to the source of this music, until I dipped and kissed Jill and one of my groomsmen reached into his pocket, pulled out a red cape, and placed it over my back and around my neck. As I carried Jill out of the church to the Superman theme, everyone in the auditorium figured out exactly what was happening. They were witnessing the birth of a supernatural marriage!

No one would have guessed that *Kryptonite* would fall into our laps just three and a half years later.

| MILE |

**"This is true love—You think this comes
around everyday?"
— Westley, *The Princess Bride***

While most couples will agree that the first year of marriage is the hardest, Jill and I learned quickly how to communicate with maturity and honesty, therefore bypassing a lot of that early marital tension. However, reaching out to youth through an effective life-on-life style of ministry often required us to have constant availability to the callings of middle school and high school kids, an impact that often challenged us as newlyweds.

After about a year and a half of doing this youth ministry as a married couple, I received a call from Pastor Mike Hays in Oklahoma City, asking me if I would consider moving there to start a Christian camp for inner-city youth on a 47 acre piece of wooded land that they had set aside. (This request made sense since I had worked for several summers at "Kids Across America," an amazing Christian camp for inner-city kids in the Missouri Ozarks, three summers as Assistant Director.) The timing of Pastor Mike's call amazed Jill and I as we had recently told our Dallas youth ministry board that this would be our last school year there, and that we would be looking for something different. I hadn't yet even prepared my resume', and in came this call. As a Christian, I couldn't help but think of a few applicable Scriptures, and our Lord's faithfulness to look after His own:

Trust in the LORD with all your heart and lean not on your own understanding; in all your ways acknowledge him, and he will make your paths straight.
Proverbs 3:5-6 (NIV)

See, I have placed before you an open door that no one can shut.
Revelation 3:8a (NIV)

Even though these Scriptures make God's care and provision clear, I'd be lying to say that Jill and I felt no stress about the move to Oklahoma City. Generally, I've learned that in matters of faith, it's one thing to *know* something; it's a completely different matter to *feel* it and wholeheartedly believe it. This is especially challenging since faith, the Bible tells us, is "the assurance of things hoped for, *the certainty of things not seen*" (Hebrews 11:1). It wasn't any easier, practically speaking, that Jill was also in the middle of her pregnancy, Oklahoma City was a three hour drive away, and we didn't have any family or friends there. But as people of faith, we knew we were trusting in an extremely reliable Source; so we planned and prepared for the move with hopeful hearts and optimistic attitudes.

As you can imagine, we were elated about the arrival of our coming little one, whose gender we kept a surprise. Of course, we did numerous pre-baby arrival things, including name selection. If our baby was a boy, we would name him Josiah, after one of the greatest kings in the Old Testament (2 Kings 23:25), who had become king as a boy and courageously brought about revival among God's people, reminding them of His written Word. Josiah, Scripture tells us, was also a man of compassion and kindness, in addition to this tremendous revival he led (Jeremiah 22:16). And if our baby was a little girl, we planned on naming her Danielle, with the nickname, "Dani," after my middle name, Daniel.

I'm sure those nine months seemed like a million years to Jill, who fought terrible nausea for almost the entirety of her pregnancy, but finally in early September, she gave birth to a precious, healthy little girl. The delivery happened just after midnight, and Jill was understandably exhausted. As she was falling asleep, I asked her if she was certain about the naming of our new daughter. When I raised the question, Jill noticed what I was thinking, that our little girl didn't really look like a "Dani." Jill then asked me if I had any other options in mind.

Knowing that we both wanted to name our child after a biblical character, I had earlier considered the name Abigail (1 Samuel 25), or Abby, which in the original Hebrew means "source of joy" or "the father's joy." I told Jill this idea and its meaning, and she thought it had a wonderful value for this child's sense of worth, and it was also cute and a good fit for her. So we agreed upon our child's name in this thirty second conversation.

At about that time, the youth camp was also beginning, and I gave it a biblical name as well. I decided to call it, "Shiloh" (Joshua 18), which means "place of peace," indicating the rest and refuge that I wanted us to offer our campers from inner-city environments. Honestly, though, I myself needed some of that peace, as it seemed that everything important in my life was just *beginning,* and I was extremely nervous about starting fatherhood, not to mention how I felt about directing a brand new camp that we had created from the ground up. Truly, both seemed like probable failures to me.

At this time, I actually reconsidered that popular Scripture passage that I mentioned earlier. In this situation, I was so glad to have it memorized—literally on my heart and mind at a necessary time:

> *Trust in the LORD with all your heart and lean not on your own understanding; in all your ways acknowledge him, and he will make your paths straight.*
> Proverbs 3:5-6 (NIV)

I began to look to God as the trustworthy One who could and would help me as I attempted to charter new and unfamiliar territory both in my personal and professional life.

As for parenting Abby, that first year with her was far easier than I could have imagined, mainly because Jill was such a fantastic mother to her, and I was her partner in what we felt was a fun process. Our marriage was still relatively new, and we regularly found ways to work together to solve the challenges that would present themselves with baby Abby or with life in general.

Shiloh's first year was also a tremendous blessing with an amazing staff of counselors and several weeks of kids who experienced an incredibly fun time while simultaneously hearing the Gospel and playing. Numerous kids came to understand Christ's saving grace inside the gates of Shiloh, and I even baptized one camper boy at his church home who came to Christ at our camp that first summer.

Certainly, my relationship with God deepened in the year 2000, which was Abby's birth year and Shiloh Camp's first year, largely because I became more reliant upon Him and found Him to be trustworthy and reliable. In a somewhat similar fashion, Jill and I also grew closer to one another that year as we depended upon each other in almost every waking (and sleeping) hour when we were both home. For that reason, we fell deeper in love.

Abby turned one a few months before we celebrated Christmas in 2001. Not long after that, Jill learned that her grandfather passed away, and his funeral would be near Beaumont, TX. I remember Jill feeling very sad about this. Being a Texan, she referred to her grandparents as "Mammaw and Pappaw," and she truly loved them both very much. She called her parents and brother a few times for information and, we made plans to attend Pappaw's funeral.

Initially, Jill and Abby and I drove to Temple, TX and stayed with Jill's parents. Jakie and Dottie Shirley always exuded such warmth and grace to me that I looked forward to our visits with them. It was a shame that feelings of grief shadowed our thoughts during this stay, but the Shirley's were as hospitable as they had ever been.

I recall sending an email to some church friends in Oklahoma City that evening from Temple, asking them to pray for Jill's family given the loss of their dear Pappaw. Ironically, I closed my email with 1 Corinthians 15:55, which says:

"Where, O death, is your victory? Where, O death, is your sting?" (NIV)

| MILE |

"That'll leave a mark."

The next morning, January 15th, 2002, we drove to Houston, to pick up Jill's brother, Jon, at Houston Hobby Airport, and we all ate lunch together before trekking down Highway 10 into Beaumont. Shortly after lunch, I was driving with Jakie sitting next to me, Jon behind him, and Jill behind me with Abby between her and Jon. We struggled against severe winds that were rocking our vehicle, making it difficult even to keep the car on the highway. I found myself fighting for control of my vehicle.

I don't remember what happened next, but I'm told that a strong gust of wind forced my car onto the shoulder of the highway. Somehow, as I attempted to correct our small SUV's shift, it began to roll. It flipped five times, crossed the median, and was hit by a tractor-trailer truck.

Jill *died instantly*.

Miraculously, Abby didn't have a scratch on her little body. In fact, witnesses say that my child never even cried. My fate, however, seemed much worse. Evidently, my skull cracked open, my neck was severely jarred, and part of my brain (literally) fell out and was on my sleeve. No one expected me to live through the night, and there was the fear that my daughter would end up "little orphan Abby." Jakie and Jon both suffered less severe injuries, *physically* that is.

> ### MILE
>
> **"If love is the answer, could you rephrase the question?"**
> **—Lily Tomlin**

I loved Jill so very much, but after 3½ years of happy marriage, that just didn't seem to matter anymore. It no longer mattered that I had held out until I was 27 years old, looking for exactly the right kind of girl to marry, and she was perfect! It no longer mattered that we were the perfect team for the creation of a sports and arts centered youth camp. It didn't matter that she could sing and I could preach, that together we made a strong ministry force. She was gone now. Instantly, she had been snatched away, and my spirit was crushed.

I should say my spirit *would be* crushed, because at that time, my skull had literally been crushed, and it would take five weeks in that local hospital in Beaumont, TX before I would be of right mind to think correctly and recall enough details to understand that my beloved wife had died, and the significant impact that that event would have on mine and Abby's lives for the days to come.

> ### MILE
>
> **"Go to jail. Go directly to jail. Do not pass go, do not collect $200."**
> **—Monopoly (Parker Brothers)**

The Rescue

"I believe in the sun even when it is not shining,
in love even when I'm alone, and in God
even when He is silent."
—Found scratched on a concentration camp wall

> **"God is our refuge and strength,
> an ever-present help in trouble."
> Psalm 46:1 (NIV)**

God is good.
All the time!
All the time.
God is good!

This slogan found its way into churches worldwide several years ago. I myself heard and repeated it countless times, and I never doubted the message it conveys. God is good and He's good all the time. I believed this, but did I truly understand it or really consider all that it might entail?

I've heard many preachers speak of the Lord's faithfulness and the consistent mercies bestowed upon His people. I have even read Jesus' promise in Scripture assuring me that He is always at work (John 5:17). But did I really grasp this deep down?

It is one thing to know and respond to popular Christian recitations. And you can even read and be inspired by the wisdom of Scripture. But when your car flips five times, your wife dies, your head splits open, and part of your brain is on your sleeve, you'd better hope that you can take those things to the bank. What happened in January of 2002 certainly left me with some questions and frustrations, but it also clarified that everything I had ever heard and read about God being "good all the time" was, in fact, as true as the sky is blue. My opinion of God—His gracious, rescuing nature—and my relationship with Him was forever reshaped and solidified on that fateful day.

MILE

**"Here on earth you will have many trials and sorrows.
But take heart, because I have overcome the world."
John 16:33 (NLT)**

No one could have guessed or foreseen God's sovereign initiative to miraculously save my life. Literally, as soon as my car began to crash, God began working. He put a gentleman at the scene whose watch was slow, who had never been that way home before, and who had military-medical training to treat brain injuries. In other words, he should not have been at that place, at that time, and he certainly shouldn't have known exactly what to do to maintain my well-being, to bring emergency care to my fractured skull and injured brain.

Yes, by what I now call a "God-cidence," Sergeant Troy Dick was present, having seen the accident in his rear view mirror. He quickly ran across Highway 10, first checked about doing CPR on Jill whom he discovered had already passed, and then assessed my situation.

Sergeant Dick first moved Abby, who was still in her baby seat (and just looking around sucking her thumb, not even crying), in front of me. As he worked, he reminded me of why I needed to live, especially for this child, in order to be her parent. As he made a compress out of clothes from my spilled suitcase, he kept speaking to me and telling me all I had to live for.

After Troy's care, the sickened EMTs arranged my helicopter flight to the nearest hospital in Beaumont, TX. A neurosurgeon awaited me at Christus St. Elizabeth. His name? Dr. *Angel* (literally). Using earthly hands guided by The Great Physician, Dr. Angel operated, putting 28 titanium plates and screws in my head. The amazing doctors also immediately set to work reconstructing my face, since it had been so severely damaged. Unquestionably, Immanuel—"God with us" (Isaiah 7:14, Matthew 1:23), was actively doing His job, being Himself, and coming to my aid, working at the scene on Highway 10 and in a hospital in Beaumont, TX.

Those were my only surgeries, and I never went into a coma. What would follow in the next five weeks were hours and hours of occupational and physical therapy, aimed at my restoration, in hopes of answering the question, "Is Jason still in there somewhere?" I also slept in a bed those days which was surrounded by a netting cage, evidently for my own safety.

My faithful mom got minimal sleep those nights for the five weeks that I was in the Beaumont hospital, as she sat bedside and looked after me. She tells stories of "baby steps" that I took that would renew her hope. For example, one day on a walk inside the hospital, I simply stopped off at a drinking fountain, pushed the button, and leaned over for a drink. It may not seem like a big deal at all, but given the severity of my injury, my mom was just *thrilled* that I knew what a water fountain was for and how to use it. On another day, she recalls that I gave her another thrill when I tied my own shoes.

An astonishing medical miracle (that part of my brain fell out, yet I was recuperating so quickly) was taking place that would confuse my neurologists and encourage the other patients at that hospital in Beaumont, TX. Yes, God's grace was evident there, even though it had certainly shown up in disguise, it was very present.

X-Ray of Jason's head after neurosurgery

"Trouble is all around me, but you keep me alive."
Psalm 138:7a (NIrV)

I don't remember anything about those first weeks in the hospital. Though I made many improvements, I still struggled with some basic tasks and functions. One of those was my ability to remember details. This brought about much frustration, but it also provided a bit of comic relief.

I'm told that one afternoon my main trauma surgeon, Dr. Parkus, was making his rounds and stopped to check on me. He struck up a conversation, intending to check on my orientation ability, or how "with it" my functioning was about a week or two since the accident and head injury.

"What's your name?" He asked.

"Why do you ask?" I shot back, apparently in a very frustrated mood. I didn't feel like talking. Besides, Dr. Parkus *knew me.*

"Oh, just want to see how you're doing today and call you by name as part of our conversation.

My friend, Bruce Bockus, who was visiting my room at the time, tells me that I grew very irritated and I answered in an agitated huff, "My name is Betty. Betty Smith." Why I chose that name is baffling to me, but it brought about smiles and laughs in a very difficult time.

Such smiles frequented my hospital room in the midst of this horrid tragedy, because I was blessed with numerous friends who stopped by to visit. Since I had been a youth minister in Dallas for five years, many of those kids were now in Texas colleges and were glad to road trip to Beaumont to come support me.

Another friend named Todd Rapp came to visit me briefly during my hospital stay in Beaumont, and when he walked in, I quickly responded, "Hey Rapper!" My mom later asked me how I knew him and could say his name. I reminded her that Todd and I were close buddies, and we had been roommates for two years in Dallas. We were co-leaders of the aforementioned youth ministry. My mom had endured countless nights of only two or three hours of sleep while caring for me; with a look of disbelief on her face, she replied, "I've been your mom for 30 years!"

Looking back, I of course feel terrible about this conversation. But thankfully, like many other abnormal behaviors that I displayed those days, my mom didn't take this conversation as a personal insult. Instead, she was glad that I showed any positive recall at all!

During this time, while I couldn't remember my own name, and couldn't even remember my own mother, something unbelievable happened, something that could only be attributed to the God of the universe.

According to the doctors and friends present, I'm told that I sat up one day in my hospital bed and told everyone that I would be preaching on Sunday. When laughter subsided, they asked me what I would preach about, to which I quickly replied, "Jeremiah 29:11." Although my memory had lost several other intimate things, it still held tight to that particular Biblical reference, to a verse which says,

"'For I know the plans I have for you,' declares the LORD, 'plans to prosper you and not to harm you, plans to give you hope and a future.'"

So even though I could barely walk, I was actually wearing an adult diaper, and I thought my name was "Betty," the Creator and Restorer Himself put His Word on my mind, specifically about how He had a *plan to give me a good hope and a bright future.* I'm living out that future right now.

MILE

"It's always darkest before the dawn."
—Author Unknown

David, the biblical shepherd boy who was anointed as God's chosen king, wrote most of the Psalms about 3000 years ago. Psalm 23, often referred to as "the Shepherd Psalm," describes the Lord as a Shepherd. David states, "Even though I walk through the valley of the shadow of death, I will fear no evil, for you are with me" (Psalm 23:4, ESV). He does not say, "I will fear no evil, because evil only happens to people who deserve it, and

I don't deserve it." He also doesn't say, "The world isn't really all that difficult; so I don't need to worry about facing evil."

No, this is the same David who as a young boy faced a nine-foot tall giant in a one-on-one battle to the death. Right before that encounter, he told King Saul, "The LORD who delivered me from the paw of the lion and from the paw of the bear will deliver me from the hand of this Philistine" (1 Samuel 17:37, ESV). Because of his faith in God's power, David faced Goliath without fear. Though the danger was still present, David trusted in a living God to enable him, to carry him through, and to give him victory.

In a more modern example, Olympic runner Derek Redmond was determined to win a medal in the 400 meter race at the 1992 Olympic Summer Games in Barcelona. Favored to make the finals, Redmond sprinted down the backstretch, only 175 meters away from the finish line. Suddenly, he pulled up lame, having torn his right hamstring. Dropping to his knees, Redmond crawled for a few seconds, his face revealing excruciating pain. Then, slowly and painfully, Redmond dragged himself to his feet and began hopping on one leg before dropping again to the track. As he lay there, clutching his right leg, a medical personnel unit ran toward him. His father, Jim Redmond, seeing his son in trouble, raced down from the top row of the stands, sidestepping people, bumping into others. He had no credential to be on the track, but none of this mattered. He just had to get to his son.

On the track, Redmond knew his dream of an Olympic medal was gone. Tears streamed down his face. As the medical crew arrived with a stretcher, Redmond told them, "There's no way I'm getting on that stretcher. I'm going to finish my race." Then, in an iconic sporting moment that millions remember, Redmond lifted himself to his feet, ever so slowly, and started hobbling down the track. The other runners had already finished the race and now watched their competitor and friend with tears in their eyes. Everyone quickly realized Redmond wasn't dropping out of the race, but was instead continuing on one leg. He was going to attempt to hobble his way to the finish line, all by himself, all in the name of pride and heart.

Jim Redmond, still desperately running to aid his son, finally reached the bottom of the stands. He climbed over the railing, head-faked a security guard, and ran out to his child. "That's my son out there," he yelled back to security, "and I'm going to help him." Finally, with Derek refusing to surrender and painfully limping along the track, Jim reached his son at the final curve, about 120 meters from the finish, and wrapped his arm around his waist. "I'm here, son. We'll finish together." Derek put his arms around his father's shoulders and sobbed. Together, arm in arm, father and son finished the race, with 65,000 people cheering, clapping and crying, witnessing what could be called a modern version of the gospel.

Scripture tells us that God is "the author and *finisher* of our faith" (Hebrews 12:2), and that "He who began a good work in you will carry it on to completion..." (Phil. 1:6). More importantly than anything else, this Olympic race pictured God, the loving Father, genuinely looking out for His children in the rough times of life's trials.

MILE

Course he isn't safe. But he's good.
He's the King, I tell you.
—Mr. Beaver, describing Aslan[3]

---

3   C.S. Lewis, *The Lion the Witch and the Wardrobe* (New York. NY: HarperCollins, 1978), Ch.8.

As I mentioned in the beginning of this chapter, the accident would leave me with some unanswerable questions, hurts, injuries, and heartaches. However, I would also grab the same truths that David and Derek Redmond understood firsthand: belief in a father that is more loving, active, faithful, and trustworthy than I had ever previously conceived. I learned to "trust God's heart, when you can't trace His hand."[4]

Obviously, I did not learn these lessons quickly or easily. Rather, the school that taught me about these riches of God's grace was lengthy and painful. But, while I hated the process, I am certainly grateful for the results.

MILE

"The Lord is good, a strong refuge when trouble comes. He is close to those who trust in Him."
Nahum 1:7 (NLT)

---

4   John McLaughlin, *Trusting God's Heart When You Can't Trace His Hand* (New York, NY: Ragged Edge Press, 1999)

Picking Up Again

Rehabilitation balance beam

"A man barely alive. We can rebuild him."
—The Six Million Dollar Man

We can never see the sunrise by
looking toward the west.
—Japanese proverb

I n the opening scenes of *Batman Begins* (2005), a young
Bruce Wayne falls down an abandoned shaft and breaks
his leg. After his father finds him and carries him out,
Dr. Thomas Wayne asks, "Why do we fall down, Bruce? So
we can learn to pick ourselves up again."[5]

---

5   *Batman Begins.* Warner Bros. Pictures, 2005.

As a superhero fan, I was thrilled by this movie release and particularly by this moment in the young Bruce Wayne's early life. I knew that the filmmakers were intentionally using such a scene to play a role in creating a strong survival instinct in their crime fighting hero, Batman. I begin here with this narrative because I took a severe fall in multiple ways: physically, mentally, socially, emotionally, and spiritually. It's important to understand how I, like the young and wounded Bruce Wayne, was also gently and lovingly picked up. Again and again, the Lord picked me up through His people and most especially through my amazing and unwavering family.

I spent roughly five weeks in the hospital in Beaumont, Texas. Those days included a grueling prescription of physical and occupational therapy for hours each day. I slept inside a netted bed at night for my own protection, with some form of restraining devices that I would occasionally "Houdini" my way out of, which was baffling to my nurses and therapists. One day, they questioned my mom about my background, and when she told them that I had been a successful wrestler, they suddenly understood my occasional escapes from the bed restraints.

When it appeared that I was ready to move forward, my neurologists agreed to my release, and I left with my parents to their home in St. Louis, MO. Though I had been living independently for a decade and my own home was in Oklahoma City, it was apparent that I had quite a road ahead of me before I could possibly handle abiding alone again. On top of learning to function independently, I also needed to learn to care for Abby... alone.

It was humbling, as a 30 year old, to realize my need to live like a ten year old again. Because my brain injury was so extensive, I had to work harder to accomplish everyday tasks. This, along with my prescribed medication, resulted in severe fatigue. I napped every afternoon and went to bed each night by 8:30. My mom faithfully encouraged me to read for a length of time each day, an exercise recommended by my neurologist. Reading was a good "brain exercise," something I needed to do daily for a neurological "workout," as part of the process that would restore all my proper brain functions.

I now understand that my body, both mentally and physically, has been graced with archives, or its own storage banks. In other words, my muscles, my coordination, and my balance all had memory, as did my different mental and scholastic capacities. So things came back to me in a *relearning* season; they were *not lost* even though I'd experienced a traumatic brain injury. They just had to be brought back to the forefront, even things like historical facts or math problems.

And the same is true for physical functions. One day I asked my dad if I could try some wrestling moves again carefully. Along with my brother one afternoon, I drilled (or practiced) a dozen different moves as I had done for many years of my younger life. They had not been lost; I simply needed a reminder. I still think that's remarkable.

MILE

"Reading is to the mind what exercise is to the body."
—Richard Steele

At this time, my folks had arranged for Abby to spend weekdays with my Aunt Pat and Uncle George, also in St. Louis, and weekends with us. Their intent was for Abby to be easily accessible and nearby, but they also knew about my fatigue levels from my recovery phase. I was nowhere near prepared for fatherhood. Aunt Pat and Uncle George are very dear people, so kind and loving, and were such wonderful caregivers to Abby at this necessary time. (When the accident first occurred, Abby stayed with Jill's parents in Texas.)

Within the first few days of my return to St. Louis, I learned the painful news of Jill's death. Though no one had officially told me before, I wasn't totally surprised. I must have either heard somehow previously, or else I figured out that if she was alive and okay, she would have been by my side by that point.

At this time, I felt this sickening mixture of physical and emotional pain. On one hand, my head and neck were in a constant straight of soreness, such that it even hurt to turn my head to the side. On the other hand, I was a young widower, a man who had been married for over three years, now forced to learn to cope with the loss of my wife, my partner, my lover, my best friend.

Add to the mix the *very* important factor of how my emotions would affect my baby girl as she began to grow up without a mommy by her side. I realized all of this, and it was honestly overwhelming.

I sat with my parents and brother in their living room and watched a video recording of Jill's funeral shortly after they told me the dreadful news. She was buried while I fought for my life. I cried. When it was over, I wanted to watch it again, and I cried again. Then I told my parents that was enough. I didn't need to see it anymore. I didn't want to watch it ever again.

It's difficult to articulate the mix of emotions that fed into my atypical brand of mourning. As I simultaneously dealt with substantial physical pain and emotional pain, I also recognized the need to strengthen my emotional health quickly for the sake of my child who had only one living parent. The weight of the world was on my shoulders, and I found myself regularly leaning upon the mighty One for emotional and physical strength. While my struggles were almost unbearable, I knew that I would soon be raising Abby alone, and that was most important. I needed to face that growing little girl regularly with *gladness*, not with *madness* or *sadness*. Only the living God could enable me to do that in my state.

After the funeral video, and the emotional pain and strain that I began to endure due to Jill's early passing, I suffered a serious emotional fall. But despite my fragile state, I know sweet little Abby needed me to "pick myself up," or better yet, let *God Himself divinely pick me up*, restore me, and give me a heart of gladness, especially for her sake. She fed off my emotions so there was little time to wallow in my grief. I began to pray and ask. It didn't take long for me to be reminded of what He told His people through Nehemiah a few thousand years ago: "The joy of the Lord is your strength" (Neh. 8:10, NIV). Truly, God began to lessen my feelings of mourning due to my specific concerns for Abby. I will revisit some questions and concerns regarding my own personal deep grieving and God's role in that later.

MILE

"O Lord... Restore me to health."
Isaiah 38:16 (ESV)

Alongside the road to emotional well being, I also labored toward *physical* wellness. This required regular sessions with a physical therapist named Chris. She gave me various neck exercises, and explained to me that when I did them I would feel a certain amount of "discomfort" (i.e. pain), but Chris assured me that I was not injuring myself any worse. Rather, working through the pain, in my case, was a necessary part of my healing process.

Chris was shocked, I recall, that I was generally in a positive, upbeat mood when I went to see her. When she asked me about it, I replied that I was thankful that she was trying to help me. She was still surprised and told me that most folks were mad about their injuries or accidents, and they never did their exercises from the therapists at home.

I did mine regularly, largely because I tore my rotator cuff fifteen years earlier in high school wrestling, and had done numerous rehabilitation exercises to rebuild strength in my repaired shoulder muscle. When I first began, I could only lift a can of pie filling. I trusted that the same principles would apply to my neck exercises now, since I'd learned at a young age that hard work reaps rewards. It gave me a strong shoulder.

I applied the same diligence to my neck exercises, not because I enjoyed the rehab, but because I knew it would help. Having a sour attitude and therefore not doing the exercises seemed like a double-loss to me. I hated my shoulder injury initially, but I quickly found that I could only get back on the wrestling mat if I worked diligently on my rehabilitation. And so many years later, as I worked diligently to restore my broken body to health, I found myself thanking God for the shoulder injury of my youth and the lessons I learned.

Chris also helped me in physical therapy with my balance. The accident severely impaired my balance, and I couldn't even walk across a five foot long mini balance beam. So my therapist faithfully worked with me to improve and restore my sense of balance, which had been jarred, given my head injury. (This is no longer a problem in any way today.)

In addition to my regular therapeutic appointments, my faithful father worked out with me twice-a-day for ten months, and we never, ever took a break. Without exaggeration, my dad is the most disciplined man that I know, and I'm grateful for his diligence, because he kept me on point. As we worked together, I discovered that muscles have memory. I was in fairly good shape prior to the accident, having run three marathons, and thus my body began to mend itself more rapidly and easily when it received such faithful and regular support.

Our workouts consisted of both running and weights. When we first began running, we started at a mile and a half. I wasn't able to complete this short distance without walking every few minutes. Because of my balance issues, I couldn't keep my gait completely straight while running. Instead, my dad tells me that I would occasionally move back-and-forth in an unsteady manner. Thankfully, by God's grace and by my dad's patient persistence, we were able to go for 4-5 mile loops together by the end of the 10 month period.

MILE

**"Don't give up Joseph, fight till you drop
We've read the book, and you come out on top"
—Go, Go, Go Joseph** [6]

---

6   *Joseph and the Amazing Technicolor Dreamcoat*, (M) Andrew Lloyd Weber, (W) Tim Rice; 1968.

While my dad oversaw my physical mending, my mom took over the rehabilitation of my *mental* capacities. Throughout much of 2002, she put aside her consulting job contracts to be with, and help, me. One of the ways I relearned basic facts was through her pop quizzes while we walked through the mall. She asked me questions like, "Who was Ben Franklin?" To which I replied, "Ben Franklin was a really great man as an inventor and scientist. He used a kite to figure out how to use electricity. And he was one of our American presidents."

"You're partly right," my patient mom answered, "but Benjamin Franklin was *not* a President of the United States."

I'll never forget that conversation or how difficult it was for me to understand and believe that Franklin hadn't been President. "But his face is on one of our dollar bills!" I argued. There were many instances like this, and looking back, I realize just how much I had to relearn. I'm so grateful to my mom for her persistence in helping jog my memory and pushing me along in this process of remembering facts that I had acquired over the years.

My mom re-taught me numerous common household duties, such as writing checks and balancing a checkbook, knowing that the day would soon come that I would be living alone with a small child, and I would have to be self-sufficient. She also made sure that I picked up a book and read every day for at least half an hour.

All of these tasks and others, I found out later, were things that my neurologist told her needed to be incorporated regularly into my life. They were necessary for my healthy recovery within the first year after the accident. I would later realize that not only were my dad and mom extremely kind and loving to me at this time, but they were also like my personal physical therapist and occupational therapist.

On top of that support, my brother played a significant role in helping me recover *socially*. Once a week David came over and took me to a movie. Because of my fragile, injured state of mind, I struggled with short-term memory. This made me a bit of an annoying movie partner. Nevertheless, David endured week after week. When we saw "The Bourne Identity," I became fascinated by the fact that the main character, Jason Bourne, and I shared the same name. David tells me that every half-hour I leaned over and whispered in his ear, "Ya know, his name is Jason. My name is Jason too."

Two years later, I took him with me to the sequel, and halfway through the film, leaned over and made the same remark. It was my way of saying thanks.

I also remember David willingly seeing "Jonah: A VeggieTales Movie" with me during my recovery. When we got back to my parents that evening, he referred to our ages, and then mentioned the fact that he had just willingly watched an *asparagus singing* on the big screen for a few hours. David's gentle humor helped me in a way that I certainly needed. I had to relearn how to laugh at jokes, including jokes that were even aimed at me in a fun way. This was part of the social coaching that my brother unintentionally gave me.

MILE

"Whoever said anybody has a right to give up?"
—Marian Wright Edelman

The ten months I spent in recovery with my family brought us all together like never before. Many nights we gathered together to play games, like Scrabble® or Yahtzee®. As you can imagine, such activities not only furthered my *mental* recovery by causing me to think, to strategize, and to follow rules, they also helped me *socially* by allowing me to interact with my family. We enjoyed so many laughs during those family times—like when I accidentally mixed in some "word salad" into a Scrabble® game. (Word-salad is a mixture of seemingly meaningful words that together signify nothing.)

I may have had a dysfunctional memory, but the accident had done nothing to quell my competitive drive. I sometimes made up words, insisting they were real. On one particular occasion, I created a long word containing no vowels, placed it on "Triple Word Score" squares, and challenged my mom to look it up in the dictionary. Of course, she couldn't find it, and when she told me, I responded matter of factly, "It must be because Webster doesn't know about it yet." My brother, who is even more competitive than I am chuckled and told my mom to just give me the word. "I mean, part of his brain was on his sleeve, for crying out loud," he quipped.

Three years after the accident, after all the physical and emotional therapy and recovery, and after God's miraculous healing touch, my neuropsychologist, Dr. Kristen Sands,[7] gave me an evaluation. Her several rounds of tests led her to conclude that I had "no cognitive disabilities." I honestly had difficulty writing that last sentence with dry eyes. Part of my brain had been on my sleeve, yet the doctor concluded after testing that I have *no* cognitive disabilities. Thankfully, my mind works well enough that I am able to comprehend certain concepts, but surely I'll never fathom our Lord's amazing grace.

---

7   Staff, St. John's Mercy Medical Center, St. Louis, MO.

MILE

**"When a train goes through a tunnel and it gets dark, you
don't throw away the ticket and jump off.
You sit still and trust the engineer."
—Corrie ten Boom,
Nazi Concentration Camp Survivor, Author**

David told me about a meaningful conversation we had during one of our times together. I don't even remember this conversation, but I realize how involved the Lord was in the process of interactively healing my heart and mind as well as my physical body. Evidently, I said to my brother, "Ya know, I could either be mad at God, or glad towards God."

"What do you mean?" David asked.

I replied, "Well, *mad* that He allowed the accident to happen that killed Jill, almost killed me, and injured me so badly."

"And glad?"

"*Glad*, of course, because of all the help from you, Mom, and Dad, from the doctors and nurses, the fact that Abby wasn't hurt at all, that Sergeant Dick saved my life... you know, all that stuff," I replied.

So David inquired, "Well, which are you, mad or glad?" In a matter of fact sort of way, I responded, "I'm just glad, 'cause being mad toward God is a bunch of drama, and I don't need that."

MILE

"Life is like photography.
You use the negatives to develop."
—Anonymous

Long after those weeks and months of rehab, when my health was miraculously restored to completeness and I was back to living alone in Oklahoma City with Abby, I decided to run in the Chicago Marathon, both as a fundraiser for Shiloh Camp and as a testimony to God's greatness. My dad planned to meet me at mile 20, where we would run the last 6.2 miles together.

It thrilled my heart to spot him in the crowd, but it did not surprise me a bit, of course, when my faithful father joined my pace to finish the marathon by my side. I will always remember running that last portion with him, because as we finished that run, we both knew that it represented a great deal more than just 6.2 miles, and for me it represented far more than completing a marathon. To us both, it symbolized the completion of ten months of two-a-day workouts, and the payoff they yielded was a physical life fully recovered.

Hallelujah!

MILE

"The best way out is always through."
—Robert Frost

Faith to be Strong[9]

Give us faith to be strong
Father, we are so weak
Our bodies are fragile and weary
As we stagger and stumble to walk where You lead
Give us faith to be strong

CHORUS:
Give us faith to be strong
Give us strength to be faithful
This life is not long, but it's hard
Give us grace to go on
Make us willing and able
Lord, give us faith to be strong

Give us peace when we're torn
Mend us up when we break
This flesh can be wounded and shaking

---

8   Courtesy of Marathonfoto.com
9   Lyrics by Andrew Peterson, music by Andrew Peterson and Gabe Scott

When there's much too much trouble for one heart to take
Give us peace when we're torn
CHORUS

Give us hearts to find hope
Father, we cannot see
How the sorrow we feel can bring freedom
And as hard we try, Lord, it's hard to believe
So give us hearts to find hope

CHORUS

Give us peace when we're torn
Give us faith, faith to be strong

Back to the
Twin Bed

**"You have taken away my companions and loved ones.
Darkness is my closest friend."
—Psalm 88:18 (NLT)**

**"Loneliness is the most terrible poverty."
—Mother Teresa of Calcutta**

A s mentioned earlier, my heart and soul also underwent some emotional and spiritual therapy during my recovery time in St. Louis. Yes, I *generally* chose gladness over madness, as I knew I should, but it's fair to say that just as my body's healing process was exactly that, a lengthy *process,* so was my emotional restoration. It certainly was not immediate, even though sweet Abby thankfully would have never guessed otherwise.

Yes, I intentionally minimized this for her sake, but I ached inside with feelings of sorrow and loneliness that were equivalent to the physical pain from which my neck and head were recovering. These emotions were accentuated when just the two of us began our new existence together upon our return to Oklahoma City at the end of 2002.

Considering the first week of the world's creation, John Milton once pointed out: "Loneliness is the first thing which God's eye named, 'not good'."[10] I found that what was true in the Garden of Eden was just as true in my own personal life as well. My heart, as much as my body, desperately needed repair and rehabilitation. I needed to somehow learn to improve my own personal well-being and functioning ability, while simultaneously relearning how to parent my child, and parent her *alone*. All of this had to happen while I adapted to this heart-wrenching grief from being widowed after only three years of marriage. The reality recognized by Milton and claimed by the Lord Himself was becoming a vast, cavernous hole inside my heart.

Perhaps the most painfully emotional reality happened every night when I went to bed. I had grown used to sleeping next to my wife in our double bed, but now the bed was half-empty. I still didn't feel right hogging part of Jill's side, so, as I continued to sleep in this half-empty double bed alone, I just stayed on my side. Of course, I sometimes wished in half-awake (and in wide-awake) moments for her to be there next to me for a sweet or gentle touch. The reality of her absence finally became so dreadful that what seemed

---

10   *The Prose Works of John Milton*, p. 181, specifically referencing God's creation account in Genesis 2:18.

best and most healthy was for me to simply change to a twin bed.

In addition to learning to sleep alone, I also had to deal with the loss of a tradition that seemed fairly insignificant, but that became a terrible pain, deep in my soul. Besides the fact that my wife was no longer next to me to hold, to talk with, or to keep the bed warm, our nightly tradition of staying up and watching late episodes of *Frazier* also died on that January day. In fact, watching what had once been one of my favorite shows became so painful that I would never watch it again. Occasionally I thought about it, but I always ended up pulling the sheets up over my head and going to sleep alone.

There were countless other memories that I missed about Jill and our relationship. She often sang while doing regular things around the house. She played with Abby in a way that usually made our daughter laugh. And Jill had a simple but very strong faith in a God that she was absolutely certain was reliable.

I was lonely, sad, and angry. It may seem absurd, but inside my heart I had completely moved beyond any gladness toward God now that my mind was beginning to process things normally and becoming more operational. Honestly, I was starting to wrestle with thoughts and doubts inwardly, and I found myself angry with God. After all, *He is all knowing, all loving, and all powerful, yet He allowed such a horrific thing to happen.*

Unanswerable questions churned in my head: God could have prevented what happened on the afternoon of January 15th, 2002. Why didn't He keep our tires on the ground and push the semi over a little? He who parted the Red Sea[11] and

---

11   Exodus 14.

caused city walls to fall[12] could have prevented our car from crossing that median. My wife died, and I was left not only emotionally injured, but with drastic physical wounds as well. I wanted to trust Him, but could I? And if so, how?

"I Still Haven't Found What I'm Looking For" [13]
—Bono

One afternoon, about five months into my recovery, I told my mom about part of my anger with God, the part that had to do with me living like a ten year old again. I hesitated to tell her about my deep grief and loneliness, as I didn't believe that *anyone,* even my mom, could ever understand my horrid aches.

"I don't like living this way," I said. "I just want to move back to Oklahoma City with Abby and begin living like an adult again."

"I'm sorry you feel that way," She replied, "But your neurologist said that you need to remain with us doing therapy for at least ten months in order for complete healing to take place."

Mom then encouraged me to pray through my feelings of anger. I began to pray about exactly that, as she suggested. Within just a few days, I actually came across a reference that says, "The king's heart is in the hand of the LORD; he directs it like a watercourse wherever he pleases." (Proverbs 21:1, NIV) In my grief and mourning, I asked God to steer my heart in a

---

12   Jericho, Joshua 5:13-6:27.
13   U2, *I Still Haven't Found What I'm Looking For—The Joshua Tree* (New York, NY: Island Records, 1987), CD.

happier direction, to change my feelings from frustration to ones of gladness.

After a couple more days of uttering this guttural prayer, I came across a Biblical story about someone in a situation somewhat similar to mine. John the Baptist, Jesus' cousin and forerunner questioned if Jesus was the promised one (the Christ). Though he had previously referred to Christ as "the Lamb of God, who takes away the sin of the world" (John 1:29, ESV), John now questioned Jesus' identity and role when he himself was imprisoned, and his own expectations were severely let down. Jesus sent His disciples to John's to report on some of His work, and to simply say, "Blessed is the one who is not offended by Me" (Matthew 11:6, ESV).

It shook me when I read this passage and specifically that last statement, because I felt as if Jesus was speaking directly to me. Suddenly, I realized that what *really* mattered had a lot less to do with my personal situation, and a lot more to do with matters of God's workings. Similarly, John the Baptist was supposed to understand that his question, "Is Jesus the One?" did not hinge at all upon the outcome of his personal trials or imprisonment. These realizations caused my heart of offense towards God to severely lessen. God, in fact, did change and steer my heart, as His word indicated He would, and my anger toward Him began to subside.

MILE

**"The bud may have a bitter taste,
But sweet will be the flower."
—William Cowper[14]**

---

14   *God Moves in a Mysterious Way*, William Cowper, 1774.

I also learned to stop asking "Why?" This lesson came to me through Job, a man who suffered tremendous pain, grief, and sorrow, perhaps more than any other single individual all at once. God never gave Job an explanation for his numerous sufferings. As readers, we have distinct insight that Job did not possess. We know the circumstances, but Job did not.

Job certainly sought answers to his pain through verbal communication with the Lord. Yet God left Job wondering why he had to face so much adversity and misfortune. Have you ever stopped to think about God's intentionality in refusing Job an explanation? The Lord intended to teach Job even greater things from the pit of despair.

Through faithful and deep study of this book, I realized that perhaps God had something of more profound significance to teach me. Perhaps I would better understand the "fellowship of sharing in His sufferings."[15] It also occurred to me that I might be in store for even greater healing *inside,* a healing that would enable me to be a healing source for others.

The book, The Wounded Healer[16], by Henri Nouwen gave me a story that further confirmed this in my heart. The story comes from the Talmud in which a rabbi asked Elijah when the Messiah would come. "Go and ask him yourself," Elijah replied. "Where is he?" asked the rabbi. "Sitting at the city gates," Elijah told him. "How shall I know him?" the rabbi wondered. "He is sitting among the poor covered with wounds," said Elijah. "The others unbind all their wounds at the same time and then bind them up again. But he unbinds his wounds one at a time and binds it up again, saying to himself, 'Perhaps I shall be needed. If so, I must always be ready so as not to delay for a moment.'" This last statement, which indicates the Messiah's readiness to help those in need

---

15   Phillipians 3:10.
16   Henri Nouwen, *The Wounded Healer* (New York, NY: Doubleday Dell Publishing Group, 1979).

of His assistance, although wounded himself, is the key point of the allegory upon which Nouwen based this entire book.

Without exaggeration, after reading <u>The Wounded Healer</u>, I was certain that God had called me to be a "wounded healer" to others, that He had enabled me to *empathize* with anyone feeling hopeless, that needed new Hope, that wondered if the Lord was faithful when He seemed absent. Could my listening ear and my testimony really help such people in ways they'd not been helped before? This is when I began to recognize my circumstances not as a terrible tragedy *only*, which they were, but also as evidence of God's opening a brand new door of opportunity in my life. At this time, I began to consider going to seminary so I could become a preacher and counselor. Appropriately, the subtitle of Nouwen's book says, "In our own woundedness, we can become a source of life to others."[17]

I could personally identify with the emotional pain others felt regarding an empty chair at a holiday gathering. I now also had a greater compassion for any unmet expectations that people may have been feeling.

God also had something to teach me about Himself, His personal provision, His sufficient grace, and the place it took in the aches and pains of my life. I once heard someone say, "I have discovered that grace puddles up in wounds."[18] I came to realize that grace and pain could coexist with healing on the horizon. I also learned that out of this mix would flow a level of compassion that would certainly bring wellness, hope, and encouragement to help others endure. As I continued to pray, read, and study, I became in an odd sort of way thankful for the pain that made me more Christlike. I developed a unique understanding that the brokenhearted heal broken hearts.

---

17   Ibid, cover.
18   http://www.smokerisebaptist.org/pdfs/sermons_05/feb1305.pdf

"He comes with the grip of the pierced hand of His Son, and says—'Enter into fellowship with Me; arise and shine.' If through a broken heart God can bring His purposes to pass in the world, then thank Him for breaking your heart."[19]

My spiritual healing and development came with the knowledge that a fresh journey was on the horizon. God was calling me to not only love my daughter well and raise her right, but to share hope and healing with those around me while I was covered in bandages.

Concerning my half empty bed, I decided to buy a twin bed when we returned to Oklahoma City. It was simply too painful to sleep alone in a bed meant for two. I also got a set of both Spiderman and Batman bed sheets for it, which Abby especially liked. To go along with the sheets, I bought a Batman alarm clock that reflected up on the ceiling an actual "Bat-signal" next to the time.

On one particular night, Abby had a nightmare, and she came into my room, asking could she lie on my bed next to me for a few minutes. As we talked, she told me, "Daddy, your room is a lot cooler than mine." I replied, "No way, Abby. You have tons of awesome princess things that you like so much!" "Oh yeah," she replied. "That's true. Well, at least your *clock* is way cooler than mine." In a lighthearted way and small situation, God was already helping me be a "wounded healer" by steering my focus away from myself to my frightened daughter.

"By his wounds we are healed."
Isaiah 53:5b (NIV)

---

19   Oswald Chambers, *My Utmost for His Highest* (Uhrichsville, OH: Barbour Publishing, 1993).

"Jesus Wept."

[20]

When He went ashore he saw a great crowd,
and He had compassion on them and healed their sick.
Matthew 14:14 (ESV)

"There is no such thing as darkness;
only a failure to see."
—Malcolm Muggeridge

---

20   www.jesusweptart.blogspot.com—art   used   with   permission   by
"Horseman."

"Jesus wept." This verse (John 11:35) is popularly known for being the shortest verse in the Bible. I would also contend that it is one of the most meaningful passages in all of Scripture, largely because it accentuates divinity showing Himself to be fully human as well. It comes from an instance in which Jesus' dear friend, Lazarus, became seriously ill. Before my accident, this narrative was always one of my favorites. After Jill's death, however, the picture of Jesus weeping for a loved one resonated much more with me. I felt and identified with our Lord's emotional and practical response to grief.

In retrospect, I realize and feel a bit guilty that such tragedy and genuine grief was necessary for me to feel that the God-man, Jesus, could relate to me, since he has shown His compassion and personal concern for me in countless other ways, but this is just the honest truth. Perhaps I questioned Him like Lazarus' sisters did, as Jesus' ways and timing is certainly mysterious (Isaiah 55:8-9).

For instance, when Christ found out about Lazarus' sickness, He did not quickly come to His friend's aid, but waited two more days (John 11:6). When Christ finally arrived, Lazarus had already succumbed to death (which Jesus knew about beforehand, John 11:11). His sister Martha quickly vented her frustrations to Jesus. "Lord," she said, "if you had been here, my brother would not have died" (11:21).

Jesus' response, or lack of response, to Lazarus' illness indicated a different perspective. His answer to her questions invited her to engage in a significant paradigm shift; He asked her to consider the potential reality of resurrection. His intentions, desires, and ability were not what she assumed. In her grief, Martha's vision was skewed, and her faith was minimal, which resulted in an aggressive complaint. She left and quickly told her sister that Jesus had arrived.

Jesus found in Mary another person with unmet expectations, who did not fully realize His sovereign design. She spoke the same words as Martha in a more saddened tone, "Lord, if you had been here, my brother would not have died" (11:32, NIV). When Jesus saw her and the many surrounding her weeping, Scripture tells us that "Jesus wept" (11:35). It seems that in shared sadness, God in human form shed tears with humanity.

Shortly thereafter, the Lord did what He intended from the start. He worked a miracle and called Lazarus back from the dead. This indicates that there is a purpose in our having to endure trials. Such tests teach us greater reliance and dependence on Him, the One who knows the end from the beginning and is trustworthy and compassionate.

The apostle Paul also believed in this truth even when he had been shipwrecked, beaten, and stoned. He even referred to such happenings as "light and momentary troubles," resting in the assurance that, "though outwardly (he was) wasting away, inwardly (he was) being renewed day by day," and he just kept his eyes fixed on his unseen Lord.[21]

This *compassion* on which we can depend was a central theme of Jesus' ministry on earth, a focus of the four Gospels. The word sympathy is used rarely in the Bible, but the word compassion (which indicates *empathy)* is used extensively. Jesus always had compassion on the crowd and the people He came in contact with. He had compassion on people and *did something* about their needs. So in Christ, we see compassion defined as an *action,* or a response of kindness, mercy, or love. More specifically, in the original Greek, "compassion" in some places even meant "to have one's insides yearning," or "to suffer with (another)." Jesus' sincere, genuine, and ready compassion even further gladdens my heart and my

---

21   2 Corinthians 4:16-18

assurance that our God shares in our pain as He willingly cares for us.

> ## MILE
>
> **"You may never know that Jesus is all you need, until Jesus is all you have."**
> **—Corrie ten Boom,**
> **Nazi Concentration Camp Survivor, Author**

David said, "You have given me relief when I was in distress" (Psalm 4:1, ESV), which is a statement of thanksgiving for having been set free not *from* suffering but rather *through* suffering. Likewise, in the "Shepherd Psalm," he said, "Even though I walk through the valley of the shadow of death, I will fear no evil, for you are with me" (Psalm 23:4, ESV)." David did not say, "I don't have to worry about evil really happening," or "God, please remove evil from my life." Instead, David understood that he would face trials, but that his trustworthy God would always be by his side to help him through such times, and David's own faith would increase in the process. He was dependent upon the One whom he came to know as his Rock and Deliverer, who empowered him to defeat a lion, a bear, and a nine-foot tall giant (1 Sam. 17:36-37).

In the same way, three teen-aged boys got thrown in a life sized oven, heated seven times hotter than usual, simply because they had faith in the true God and refused to bow down to the king (Daniel 3). In the furnace, though, Scripture describes a 4th One who walked around with them, and who protected them, so much that their clothes didn't even smell like smoke. Truly, after a night of *bowling,* my clothes smell like smoke for a week, and these young men were in a burning furnace, but *God met them in their place of trial.*

MILE

**Don't ever be afraid or discouraged!
I am the LORD your God, and I will be there
to help you wherever you go.
Joshua 1:9b (CEV)**

As in any passage of Scripture, there is more than one lesson to be gleaned. I drew great strength from the biblical narrative of Lazarus through the reminder that God cries for and with me when I am heartbroken. For the first time, I began to truly understand what David meant when he said, "The LORD is close to the brokenhearted and saves those who are crushed in spirit." (Psalm 34:18, NIV) I never fathomed it before because I had never been so brokenhearted, downcast, or crushed.

I also gained new appreciation for passages that give a healthy allowance for mourning and grieving:

"Blessed are those who mourn, for they will be comforted."
Matthew 5:4 (NIV)

"There is a time for everything... a time to weep and a time to laugh, a time to mourn and a time to dance."
Ecclesiastes 3:1, 4, NIV

With this new understanding, I came to realize something that saddened my heart: Many modern churches in America are not "suffering-safe" places. In other words, if a person is hurting, he is usually treated as if he is lacking faith. The real issue, however, often has to do with fellow believers who perhaps feel uncomfortable sympathizing with the sufferer. This is where genuine compassion is lacking in today's church.

Incorrectly, many churches look more like country clubs than hospitals. Christ, the Head of the church, gave us the perfect example of compassion time and time again when He witnessed those in need and said, "It is not the healthy who need a doctor, but the sick" (Matthew 9:12, Mark 2:17, Luke 5:31). Multiple times, Scripture describes Him as "gracious and compassionate, slow to anger and abounding in love."[22] World leader, Mohandas Ghandi once said, "I like your Christ, I do not like your Christians. Your Christians are so unlike your Christ." Perhaps the lack of grace and compassion is some of the misrepresentation that Ghandi recognized.

I began this chapter by claiming that this little two-word verse that I used for this chapter's title is profound in its meaning. I will now conclude, holding to that same belief, by pointing to a declaration that begins this miraculous biblical account:

"Now Jesus loved Martha and her sister and Lazarus." (John 11:5, ESV).

It's as if the Lord is teaching us that at the very core of all His dealings with us, no matter how dark and mysterious they may be, we must dare to believe in His unmerited and unchanging LOVE. A love that dares to allow pain, yet feels

---

22   Exodus 34:6; Nehemiah 9:17; Psalm 86:15; Joel 2:13; Jonah 4:2.

our pain to the depth that we do. As I said earlier, it is wise to "trust God's heart, when you can't trace His hand."[23]

MILE

**"I will not be afraid. I will not run & hide.
For there is nothing I can't face when God is at my side."
—VeggieTales[24]**

23 John McLaughlin, *Trusting God's Heart When You Can't Trace His Hand* (New York, NY: Ragged Edge Press, 1999)
24 *Esther... The Girl Who Became Queen* (2000)

How's the Body Working?

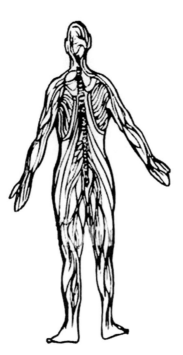

The human body

"The human body has the capacity to compensate
for a malfunctioning part."
—Woman's Passions[25]
"Its parts should have equal concern for each other.
If one part suffers, every part suffers with it...
Now you are the body of Christ,
and each one of you is a part of it."
1 Corinthians 12:25-27 (NIV)

After the accident, my physical frame was in need of repair and restoration. My walking stride lacked stability and needed some serious rebalancing. Part of my physical therapy included walking across a short balance beam. This became a daily necessity and habit. Perhaps some of the most intense suffering, however, came from the excruciating neck pain that hampered my range of motion. I endured many months of treatment at the rehabilitation center in St. Louis and faithfully performed my assigned exercises during my recovery time with my parents. And I should admit that performing these exercises was such a frustrating effort because they seemed like a massive overabundance of work accomplishing what used to be such easy, simple tasks.

People occasionally ask me what sorts of physical setbacks lingered after I completed my therapeutic recovery. My skull now has a slightly crooked shape, since it was cracked and now contains 28 titanium plates and screws. Occasionally, people ask me if the contents of my head set off the metal-detectors at airport security systems, but they do not.

On a serious note, though, my head injury did leave me with a "seizure disorder." So I daily take prescribed meds and am careful to avoid sleep deprivation.

---

25   Women's Lifestyle Magazine, Dec. 4, 2006

My *only* other physical setback is my left eye, where I am presently about 2/3 blind, mostly in the bottom half and for peripheral use. I've been told by doctors that there has been damage somewhere between the optic nerve and lens that serve that eye. Thus, I presently can hardly see downward and to the left out of that eye. That's why I ask people walking next to me to walk on my *right* side, or to sit on my right side at meals (especially my little daughter). Occasionally, I trip while walking, if objects are set down low and to the left. One time recently, I painfully cracked my left shin on the trailer hitch of a pick-up truck. At those particular moments, I hate this malfunction. Usually, though, I turn my head enough to see the things that I would miss.

What's fascinating about my eye damage is something that I now think is magnificent in its symbolism. As I began my months of treatment, I visited an optometrist as part of my necessary testing. A year later, I went back in for a routine exam. My right eye, which had already tested at 20/20, now showed a remarkable improvement. In a fascinating example of physical *compensation*, my right eye now tested at 20/15. While my left eye had been damaged, my right eye improved to *compensate* for its injury.

I've since learned that such compensation is a common practice within the human body. "In a way, the human body can be thought of as a machine. However, unlike a machine that is comprised of right angles and nuts and bolts, the human body has the capacity to compensate for a malfunctioning part, and in most cases, in more than one area. The human body seeks symmetry. It will do whatever it takes to achieve that and in doing so will compromise tissue health." In other words, "the human body is the 'great compensator.'"[26]

---

26   http://www.womanspassions.com/articles/583.html

MILE

"Alone we can do so little; together we can do so much."
—Helen Keller

The Apostle Paul compared God's people to a human body, and individuals to parts of that body, in his first letter to the church in Corinth:

The body is a unit, though it is made up of many parts; and though all its parts are many, they form one body. So it is with Christ. 1 Cor. 12:12 (NIV)

Biblically, we can see that healthy members of the church body ought to compensate for injured parts, simply because God tells us that we ought to love one another (John 13:34, 1 John 4:11), and treat others in the way we would like to be treated (Matt. 7:12, Luke 6:31). It's beautiful that this actually took place in my situation, when I was blessed with many "healthy," faithful friends who *compensated* for me in my injured position in countless ways.

For ten months of 2002, while I recovered in St. Louis, my friends in Oklahoma City regularly picked up my mail and sent it to my parents' house. Other friends in Oklahoma City mowed my grass and even maintained the upkeep of my garden. My neighbors told me about those things upon my return at the end of 2002.

Sadly, this particular call of Scripture is usually ignored by the church though. Or specifically, *injured parts* of the body of Christ are often the ones ignored by healthy members. And as I just noted last chapter, our Lord Jesus, our example, was One who was so frequently moved to action to help the people he encountered because of His *compassion* for whatever they were facing, whatever was currently injuring them.

As for my injury, I came back to Oklahoma City in December, 2002, having completed my necessary therapy, with the hope of resuming my life as I'd known it before, and my job as Shiloh Director. Each place I went, I received receptions that were generally optimistic and welcoming.

The body of believers at my home church, Britton Christian Church, intimately embraced me and actually formed a "Jason Committee," with a focused effort on assisting me. In countless ways, those loving brothers and sisters helped me and *compensated* for me, as an *injured* member of Christ's body. Talk about putting God's Word into action; these folks directly applied truths from 1 Corinthians 12 in a way that majorly benefited me and Abby.

For instance, one dear woman named Joelle cooked meals for us that lasted two years. She gave me boxes and laundry baskets full of meals, along with cooking instructions. People babysat for me whenever I needed it, and they even occasionally dusted and vacuumed our house. One man put on my kitchen counter tops, and another did some plumbing under my kitchen sink. Finally, and perhaps most importantly, they *all* prayed for us consistently.

After experiencing and receiving all these blessings, I think that my church friends must have been reading straight from James' letter that says, "Faith by itself, if it is not accompanied by action, is dead" (James 2:17, NIV). My Oklahoma City brothers and sisters went above and beyond to put faith into action for me. These healthy members of Christ's body *compensated* for me in my injured state, by showing me love, kindness, and grace in countless practical ways. What an example for all healthy members of Christ's body to follow in daily living.

MILE

"A friend in need is a friend indeed."
—English Proverb

There were, in fact, a handful of people who went the extra mile to help carry my load back to health and fatherhood. As I use this figurative language, it brings to mind the legendary "Sherpas" of the Himalayas, who have been an integral part of Everest climbing expeditions from the very beginning. "Indeed, very few significant climbing successes have been achieved without them," with their practical assistance enabling nearly every climb (by setting camp and carrying loads).

"When Western mountaineers first set their sights on the world's highest peak, they found in the Sherpas a people ideally suited to the rigors of high-altitude climbing; unfailingly positive, stout at altitude, and seemingly resistant to cold."[27]

MILE

"Carry each other's burdens,
and in this way you will fulfill the law of Christ."
Galatians 6:2 (NIV)

As I mentioned, I most certainly had some "Sherpas" along the way that helped me by carrying my loads, "setting up camp" for me regularly, and making sure I wasn't left alone

---

27 Brian Handwerk, "The Sherpas of Mount Everest," *National Geographic News* 5:10 (2002), http://news.nationalgeographic.com/news/2002/05/0507_020507_sherpas.html

on what would have seemed like an impossible task by myself. Because you see, these figurative teammates went ahead of me, seemingly tirelessly and, for sure, faithfully in their efforts, to help me *climb*, not Mt. Everest, but back to health and to raising my daughter.

In the coming pages, I will include writings from a handful of these "Sherpas" that, in major ways, assisted me in countless ways along my climb back to health, well-being, and fatherhood. As I just mentioned, God blessed me with several others as well; I'm just enclosing the written thoughts from some of my dear friends whom I asked to catalog their reflections, reactions, and responses from my accident in early 2002. And before each one, I'll give a short explanation of my relationship with that particular person.

MILE

"Friends are God's way of taking care of us."
—Marlene Dietrich

Emily Kavanaugh—Emily was my physical therapist in Beaumont, TX, who not only cared for me, helped me learn how to walk, and encouraged my parents, but she also regularly informed numerous Christian friends and Young Life leaders regarding my condition, creating a prayer chain of folks who often prayed for me. Incidentally, Emily is also one of those seen in my early post-accident walking videos, as it was her in the scrubs, helping me along.

It was January 2002—I was working as the primary therapist on the neurological floor of Christus St. Elizabeth Hospital in Beaumont, TX. I remember seeing a young man in the NICU on my morning rounds, a somewhat unusual sight to see someone so young in the ICU. His head was essentially wrapped in a headband of bandages, and I recall seeing quite a number of people surrounding his bed during the morning visiting time. I happened to see Don Joseph, who is a pastor in Beaumont and a dear friend of mine. He motioned me over to the side of the hall and asked if there was any way I could get the young gentleman in D bed on my caseload. Considering I was working on floor, I would more than likely evaluate him when the time came. Don said he went to seminary with one of the men currently standing around the guy in D bed and this man was a pastor friend of his from Oklahoma.

By Emily Kavanaugh

When I did receive a consult from Dr. Angel, Jason had been moved into a regular room on the floor. Jason still had his bandages on when I met him. There were always people in his room it seemed—and the more I was around, the more I came to learn of the amazing circle of brothers and sisters in Christ. I was a leader for Young Life in Beaumont, and 2 of the girls that were visiting Jason were staying with my area director and his wife, Danny and Shelly Williams. The group also knew of a friend of mine, Gibson Largent, with whom I worked during the summer of '95 at Camp Cho-Yeh in Livingston, TX—he attended Oklahoma Baptist University in Shawnee, OK, and Jason's wife, Jill, attended the same school.

After reviewing his history, I went in to evaluate Jason. I was only beginning to glean bits and pieces about the accident, but my focus was on seeing what Jason could do and establishing a plan for this guy. Jason could sit up to the edge of the bed with little assistance and could speak, although the words were incongruent, a "word salad". Although his eyes looked blank to me, I was surprised at how much he was speaking and interacting socially with the people present, especially given the degree of brain injury he had sustained. I met Jason's parents, Ron and Jan, and some of the other friends present. Although Ron had to fly back to St. Louis, I knew Jan kept him consistently involved in the progress of Jason's recovery. Jan and I would start on the first of many talks regarding Jason's progress and things she could work with him on in order to continue trying to get Jason's brain to make new connections. Given that someone of Jason's cognitive status responded to basic function, I figured the next day I'd "take him for a spin and see what he could do"...Jason's friends, Stephan and Bruce, were in town and had a video camera with them." Stand up...let's walk"—despite the blank look, Jason stood up and started for the door. Once in the hall, I tried to let him go at his own pace, guiding and cueing him with my gait belt to stop, turn, stand, and sit. There were fewer bandages and there was a large scar on his head covering the plate on his skull. I could look down at his arms and still see glass chards that would eventually work themselves out. Again, I was very pleased with Jason's ability to perform these basic functions. Now the challenge was in the carryover to safely perform daily tasks. Jason knows this now, so hopefully he won't be embarrassed, but the biggest task to get the catheter removed and him out of briefs was to get safely to the bathroom. (Jason will say that both he and his daughter Abby were in diapers that year.) Jan and I would coordinate so she could carry over things we found worked with Jason.

During his weeks in the hospital, I'd walk into Jason's room in the morning and tell him "hi" (and to get the report from Jan on how he did the night before). "Hi Emily" was usually followed by some comment or piece of a story or a scripture verse. I remember his laugh came back pretty quickly, too. I don't remember the exact timeline, but when he left the hospital for the rehab center, he could count to 10, walk with contact assistance, and was doing well with his balance exercises. Getting up frequently, especially during the night, continued to be a safety issue—his function was returning, but cognitively he was still very impulsive. His speech was monotone and flat, and he demonstrated little expression. My Young Life team and I continued to pray for him, and I'd keep my mom updated, too.

I went to see Jason and Jan a few weeks later at the rehab center. I walked into Jason's room and Jan reintroduced me. She was so thrilled to tell me about all the progress Jason had made. The three of us held hands and went for a walk throughout the facility. Jan would point to signs as we walked and Jason would read them for us. When we got to a long hall, Jan had him start counting to 100—by tens then fives then single digits...and he did it! His look was less blank and although he was more alert, I could tell he was not 100% Jason Mirikitani... yet. I agreed with Jan that taking Jason back to Oklahoma would be a familiar environment, and I had comfort and confidence in Jan's ability to get Jason set up. I did wonder how Jason would react when he was reunited with Abby and then resume the responsibilities eventually for caring for her.

A year later, Jan and Jason came back to Beaumont to visit. I met them on the neuro unit where Jason was being introduced to the nurses; he was also able to meet with Dr. Parkus, the trauma doctor and Dr. Angel, the neurosurgeon. Jan introduced me to Jason and we walked to my department where we could sit and visit. I was happy to see life behind his eyes and emotion behind his expressions. He laughed and joked and told me of his return to Oklahoma, and Abby and how she was growing and enjoying preschool. We looked at pictures and talked about college football. Then we started to visit about the accident and his stay at St. Elizabeth. I was willing to fill in the holes as long as he wanted to know. He did not remember the accident nor the events surrounding his hospitalization—for that I was most grateful. I had questions for Jason and Jan regarding his acclimation to life in Oklahoma. Jan said she had finally gotten Jason to get to the bathroom correctly by (brilliantly) laying Christmas lights on the floor from the bed to the toilet to guide him just like the floor lights on an airplane aisle.

That evening Jason came to talk to my Young Life Campaigner's group that had been praying for Jason during the time of his hospitalization. I remember sitting there listening to him speak, watching Jan hold Abby, realizing that "Jason Mirikitani" was back! I didn't know him before, but knew that God had restored his speech, movement, his ability to be a dad, the ability to express emotion, and had adjusted to life as a single father (and all the challenges that go along with single parenthood). He said he still had headaches, and other than the faint scar, he was back to himself. He was a walking miracle given the extent of his injuries.

I remember wondering in gross anatomy in grad school how anyone could doubt the existence of God in looking at such a fine tuned machine as the human body—with all the abilities and functions of each part. Even more amazing, how could anyone doubt a God who RESTORES, creates anew, that which is damaged, given the body's ability to heal. Jason, like each unique member in the Body of Christ, is a vessel—a clay pot especially and uniquely crafted by the Father. Taken, remolded, healed, restored. My heart grieved for the loss of Jill and sorrow that such an accident took her life. But since then, I have witnessed the healing of a husband, and the growth and joy of a daughter that God, the One on whom I know Jill relied, has provided in time.

Jason will always be one of the patients I will remember...not just for the story of his incredible healing. There was an invitation by those near and far away for God to be present to Jason. I believe God is always present—angels escorting people in and out of this world to the next—but God's peace and presence was certainly felt in that room. Jason had an innate fighting spirit and acknowledged God from the very beginning of his cognitive recovery. Jason's heart was obviously wholly dedicated to God. He was in for a long road of recovery, and I can't ignore the persistent efforts of the people that surrounded Jason.

"Oh God, my rod and my staff...help me to help Jason".

It was my joy to have the Mirikitani's up to Chicago where I was then working in October 2004. Jason had a goal to mark his full recovery and raise money for Camp Shiloh by running the Chicago Marathon. An admirable feat for anyone's undertaking, but miraculous as Jan, Ron, and I looked among the 40,000 runners for Jason at the mile markers. My heart rejoiced that this man, who had "his brains on I-10", was running with endurance, completing a testament of faith. Ron Mirikitani is a man of few words, as Jason would say, but his expressions while running the last 6 miles with Jason are priceless—you should see the pictures. I'm sure being separated physically during Jason's rehab took a toll on Ron and Jan—I've not asked them about this. However, I know that they both seek God first and foremost and lean on Him to meet all needs—He is their Rock and Foundation, Captain of their Team!

"A friend loves at all times,
and a brother is born for adversity."
Proverbs 17:17 (NIV)

Stephan Moore—Stephan is one of my all-time best friends, although we are opposite in many ways, which he actually explains in this piece. He was the Director at "Kids Across America," a Christian sports camp for inner-city kids in the Ozarks of Southern Missouri, and I was his Assistant Director for three summers. We were both in each other's weddings, and we treasure our friendship and bond with one another.

It was nearly bedtime and I was dog-tired. A long day and an evening spent with our toddler son & infant son had worn me out. The telephone blared its familiar electrical tone, but, because of the late hour, its ring was somewhat alarming. Little did I know the news that awaited me on the other end would change the life of one of my best friends forever. The voice on the phone asked if I had heard the news about Jason Mirikitani.

"No. What news?" I asked. Jason was in a terrible car accident, and Jill was killed, and Jason had a serious head injury." There's a possibility he won't make it," the voice said. Immediately my heart sank and my mind went numb. A flood of emotions swept over me... despair, sadness, loss, hopelessness and more. My mind snapped back to reality." What happened? Where? How is Abby? What is Jason's prognosis? Where did they take him?

There were few answers at this time... I had barely hung up the phone and explained what had happened to my wife when the phone rang again. It was a fellow Kanakuk director. Knowing the close friendship and brotherhood I shared with Jason, he gently said, "Steph I have some bad news to share about Jason Mirikitani... He and his family were in a fatal car wreck. Jill was killed, and it is not known if Jason will survive." I sat in silence. The tears had already begun to soak my shirt. I listened again to the limited details about the accident and Jason's condition hoping that there would be better news." No, Jill wasn't killed, that was a mistake... yeah, Jason has a bump on the head, but he'll be fine with a little rest..."

By Stephan Moore
—A Night to Remember

But no such words followed.

How had this happened? Jason and Jill were Godly people. Their passion for the Lord was authentic and sincere. They were bright, young, and had a beautiful future. ...And what about Abby? Would God really take a little girl's Mommy at such a young age? She wasn't even 2 years old!

I have long been acquainted with the truth that bad things happen to good people... But when it is so close to home, the cry of our hearts and unsanctified minds demand fairness from God. This was not fair! This was not supposed to happen! Truly, His ways are not our ways... Truly, we must not lean to our own understanding... Truly, though He slays me I will serve Him!

After a few moments to collect my thoughts and emotions I started to call some of our summer leadership team to inform them and rally them to pray for Jason and his family. Jason had served on my leadership staff at Kids Across America for several years in many roles, most recently as my assistant director. We had been friends for 10 years. An unlikely pair we had struck up a close friendship that will last a lifetime. I'm 6'8 he's 5'7, I'm African American, he has Asian ancestry, I played college basketball, he was a championship level wrestler, when I get a chance to speak, I preach hellfire and brimstone, and he is always full of grace. I grew up in the country, he grew up in the city, but somehow the Lord had forged a friendship through many opposites and given us a friendship to envy. He was loyal as my assistant director, and he was faithful as a friend who loved me enough to tell me when I was wrong or needed correction. We were in each others' weddings, and we looked forward to watching God grow us as married men with our own families... and now this!

Several days later I found myself driving to Temple, TX to Jill's funeral and then on to Beaumont to stay a few days with Jason at the hospital. As I drove through Dallas, where Jason used to live, I began to think about Jason's perspective on this. While Jason is known for his sensitivity, care and concern I knew that he would soon be looking for God's purpose in what had happened. He was and is a man of faith and tremendous trust in the Lord. He would pursue God's purpose in this. I committed myself to be a blessing and encouragement to all that I came in contact with at the funeral. That is what the Lord would do. That is how Jason would respond.

As I sat down at the funeral it seemed like only the day before, in the same church I had whipped out a bright red Superman cape to drape around Jason so that he could walk down the aisle with his new bride as the superhero that he was in her eyes! What a day that was... and now here I was with multitudes of other mourners paying my respects. The service was beautiful and rightly celebrated the life of a beautiful young woman of God who served family, friends, spouse and child with all that God had given her. Jill's brother, Jon, shared so profoundly about how Jill being the big sister preceded him in life and in the challenges and hard times that life presents. And now, she had preceded him and gone to heaven before him.

God had gifted Jill with a wonderful voice that she used to glorify Him. Shortly before the accident Jill sang "I Can See" at a church service where Jason was to preach. The video tape recording was played during the memorial service. Her voice ministered hope, healing and reassurance to the multitudes of people in that sanctuary that day. As she reached the crescendo of the song and the camera drew in for a close up on her, Jill's parents stood up lifting their hands in praise to the Lord! Wow! The place was swept with the presence of God as others stood and worshipped as Jill ministered at her own funeral. Truly, His love endures forever!

After the service I drove on to Beaumont, TX to see Jason. I had been forewarned that as handsome as he was, he didn't look so good. The latest news was that Jason's brain had been partially knocked out of his head, and that recovery was uncertain...maybe in a vegetated state or possibly limited memory of who he was or anyone else.

As I walked down the hall of the hospital toward his room, I was anxious to see my friend but unsure of just what I would see. Was he in pain? Would he recognize me? Was he grieving the loss of his wife? As I neared the door to Jason's room the obvious presence of God was emanating from the room. People were praying... you could feel it!

As I walked in the room I was greeted my Jason's mom, Jan Mirikitani. I could only imagine how she must be feeling, my words felt so inadequate. Here was her youngest son, head swollen, eyes bloodshot, hands bandaged, incoherent, and widowed with a toddler child... with only limited hope of recovery...

That's where I was wrong. If there is a story in the story, Jan Mirikitani is it! She is no ordinary woman. Small in stature and appearance, she is a towering woman of God! Always neat, cordial and kind, she is never without a twinkle in her eye and a knowing smile on her face. She invited me into the room. Obviously concerned about Jason and the loss of Jill, Jan greeted me with a big hug and many thanks for coming. She updated me on Jason's condition and outlook. Despite what the doctor's were saying, Jan's perspective was unfettered by the doctor's professional obligation to give the worst-case scenario. The faith of this woman was amazing! I'm not talking about some psychological certainty conjured up by the refusal to believe the truth and embrace reality. I'm talking about a woman of God who knows the Word of God and His promise of hope, healing and restoration. This faith coupled with a mother bear tenacity to care for her child to go with the hundreds if not thousands of people praying for Jason made this situation a legitimate candidate for a miracle! Not long after I arrived several teenagers who had been involved in the ministry that Jason used to direct arrived. After meeting each of them we stood near the entrance of the room. Suddenly I noticed one of the boys rapidly moving backwards but his feet were standing still. He fainted. Flat on his back! I wondered if Jason really looked that bad.

Jason had little recognition and his words were full of "word salad," confused collections of words from Jason's mind. Jason could hear and at times seem to respond to some questions. But he still didn't know that Jill was home with the Lord.

It was a privilege to spend the next few days serving Jason and his mom. As each day went by, it became clear that God was doing something! People seemed to be drawn to the room. Nurses and caretakers seemed to stay longer serving, talking, encouraging. Though Jason improved slowly, hope was in the air! Jason's pastor, Mike Hays, came to visit for several days. What a faithful man of God he is... He provided another voice of hope and encouragement and boost of faith. Jay Cleveland, a mutual friend of ours arrived the day before I left. I was glad someone else would be there to serve Jason and his mother. After I left Beaumont I prayed often and looked forward to the reports on Jason's progress.

The big turn of events came when Jan Mirikitani decided to take Jason home to St. Louis to continue his recovery. The doctors had been encouraging but guarded about Jason's recovery and, by all accounts, they were a wonderful team of caretakers who had served Jason and his family with their absolute best. They told Jan that taking Jason home was not a good idea...he could relapse, he could freak out in the car and on the plane. In a room, with numerous medical personnel extolling the cautions and red flags of moving Jason, Jan considered all they said but remained steadfast in her belief that Jason would do much better in a familiar environment of friends, family and surroundings to continue his recovery. Whoever said that "mother knows best" may have been right, but when an informed, Godly mother, woman of faith says she knows best, who can bet against her?!

There is more to this story that others will tell. Does God still do miracles? Absolutely! He doesn't do it all the time, but this is one story that culminates in a bonafide miracle! Praise be to God for His extension of grace to our friend Jason. My faith has increased many times over by seeing God work in Jason's life. The miracle continues!

MILE

"Nothing is impossible with God."
Luke 1:37 (NIV)

Chris Zervas—Chris, whom I usually call "Z," or "Never-Nervous-Zervas," is truly one of the most compassionate, kind-hearted guys I've ever known. He knows me as well as anyone, and I'm honored to call him my close friend. I recently and *gladly*, spent a full afternoon with my daughter and his three children at the zoo (all under age 7 at the time)! Perhaps that's an indicator of Chris' character, which is truly on the top shelf.

Jason Mirikitani is a Superman fan. We worked together for several years at "Kids Across America." During that time, he had become a Superfriend to me... like a dearly loved brother. Highlights of my summers were times off spent with Jason. We laughed, shared meals and grew very close. I was honored to be in Jason's wedding and to have him in mine. Not just because he was a dear friend. Jason introduced my wife Jenna and me.

Jason's clash with Kryptonite opened my eyes to God's great love. God's love was demonstrated by prompting me and others to be a part of His reconstruction of my friend. God used many people. My small part was prayer.

A phone call about Jason's wreck came to me late January 15th. The news that Jill died shook me greatly. But God soon gave Jenna and me great peace. I looked at her and confidently stated, "God isn't going to let him die."

The next morning I looked at my own daughter, who is a few months younger than Abby, and began begging God for Jason's life. Later that morning a very concerned Stephan Moore came by. Stephan goes 6' by 8", 250 pounds; when he began to cry, the seriousness of Jason's condition began to sink in even more.

Jenna is a physical therapist who has treated many patients with head injuries. Her knowledge led us to often pray for healing

By Chris Zervas

and protection of Jason's brain. We also prayed for God's mercy. We asked God to take Jason home if he was not going to be able to function and care for Abby.

God stirred many people like me to pray and join the Jason Mirikitani rebuilding project. Sometimes God would awaken me at night with a tremendous urging to pray for Jason. Jenna also had these middle-of-the-night stirrings.

Jason's likeability and experiences had given him relationships in so many circles. God gave this huge circle of friends (and many more who knew Jason only by reputation) a zeal to pray for his recovery.

During the months following the accident, many people asked me how Jason was doing. Even if they did not know him, they usually shared that they were praying for him. It was uncanny! These people would also share it with their church. Churches prayed. Youth groups prayed. It seemed thousands of prayers were being uttered on Jason's behalf. I have never heard about so many people praying for one man, one accident and one recovery. It was supernatural.

The fondest memory of Jason's recovery came in the spring of 2003. Stephan, Jason, Todd Rapp and I were to meet at a Chinese restaurant. I had not seen Jason since the accident. We had spoken on the phone and I detected elements of healing still happening, but was unaware of what he was going to be like, act like, or look like.

My schedule forced me to be late to the dinner. As I walked into the restaurant, my mind was preoccupied with questions. What would Jason be like? How well does he communicate? How should I act? What am I going to tell the people who ask me about him? Thinking about Stephan's humor had not crossed my mind.

There were several conversations going when I arrived; I took the opportunity to size up Jason's ability to communicate and his behavior. I hadn't reached any conclusions, but was still intent on my mission when the conversations ended. Stephan started in. "Jason, you know Z (my nickname) has a prison record and his parole officer let him come tonight to see you." Jason roared. We all roared. Stephan went on to "inform" Jason that he was actually a millionaire and before the accident he always bought everyone's dinner. The celebration had begun!

Jason Mirikitani was alive, well and in the flesh! God had done a miracle.

Since the accident, there is a slight difference in Jason. Slight. We talk often about everyday villains in our lives, his current Lois Lanes, and joke around often about his brain being out on the highway. Yet the testimony of what God has done in Jason is more powerful than a locomotive. For Jason did not just survive; he is soaring.

| MILE |

"If you fall, your friend can help you up.
But if you fall without having a friend nearby,
you are really in trouble."
Ecclesiastes 4:10 (CEV)

Bruce Bockus—I consider Bruce a big brother. He was a mentor to me in so many ways, both personally and professionally, during my time in Oklahoma City, and one of my closest friends as well. He tirelessly gave his time and efforts to the building and maintenance of Shiloh Camp, of which I was blessed to be the Founder and Director, and he also poured into my personal life as a man, a husband, and a father. I used to look forward to our early morning shared time riding the tandem bike together around Lake Hefner. I'm not surprised at all that Bruce came to the hospital to visit and support me.

January 16, 2002, Wednesday a.m.
The phone call came like an unexpected rogue wind, breaking in on the everyday activity of life, getting ready for work, the kids getting ready for school. The obviously shaken voice of John Mayfield, "Bruce, I have some tragic news about the Mirikitani's." I sat down at our breakfast room table, my mind flashed to the message I had heard from Jason the previous day, "Bruce, this is Jason and I can't ride the

tandem Thursday because Jill's grandpa died, and we are going to Beaumont, TX for the funeral, see ya bro". My mind was racing as I managed to voice a response... "John, let me have it". John replied, "Jason has been seriously injured in a car accident, he's not expected to live because of severe head trauma... Jill did not make it. Abby was not injured." The tears began immediately, my family surrounded me, and we did the only thing we could do, cry and pray. "Lord Jesus, be with your servant Jason, we commend our friend Jill into your eternal care, thank you for her life of faith. Watch over Abby..."

January 20, 2002, Sunday p.m.

Our Lord, my Lord, how majestic is Your name. My heart remains heavy, but encouraged as I witness the miraculous healing of our friend Jason Mirikitani from a tragic car accident that claimed the life of his wife, Jill. Abby was completely spared. Jason should have died, medically speaking, but, God has plans for Jason, and somehow He will be glorified through this. Lord may you make Romans

8:28 true..."That all things work together for the good of those who love you, who are called according to your purpose." Jason is _called_, thank you Lord. Amen

By Bruce Bockus

January 27, 2002, Sunday a.m.

Lord Jesus, I am making my way to Beaumont, TX to visit my dear brother in Christ, Jason Mirikitani. I have a peace about my mission, which is simply to be your conduit Lord to minister love to Jason and his mom, Jan. Lord I pray for Jason, I am encouraged by Your word this morning as I review how you are able to renew not only Jason's mind, but also my mind. Lord, fill me with your Holy Spirit once again; give wisdom generously as I visit Jason. Help me help others. I need you. You opened the eyes of your disciples on the road to Emmaus; please open Jason, healing those areas of his mind that are injured. Restore his mind; renew his mind to enable Jason to complete the tasks to which you called him. I pray these things in faith as I stand in agreement with your scripture.

Luke 24:31 "Then their eyes were opened and they recognized Him"

Luke 24:45 "Then he opened their minds so they could understand the scripture"

Luke 24:38 "Why are you troubled and why do doubts rise in your minds"

Deut. 11:18 "Fix these words of mine in your hearts and minds"

Psalm 7:9 "O righteous God, who searchers hearts and minds, bring to an end violence and make the righteous secure"

Jer.	31:33	"I will put my law in their minds and write it on their hearts"
Eph.	4:23	"to be made new in the attitude of your minds"
Col.	3:2	"Set your minds on things above, not earthly things"
Heb.	8:10	"I will put my laws in their minds"
1 Pet.	1:13	"prepare your minds for action"
Rev.	2:23	"search our hearts and minds"
Phil.	4:7	"guard your heart and mind in Christ Jesus"
Rom.	12:12	"renewing of your mind"

January 30, 2002, Wednesday a.m.

Good morning Lord! January has seemed to last for a year. It feels like so long ago since New Years Eve and then the Sooner's winning the Cotton Bowl on New Years Day. Then Lee and I went skiing with the D-team. Work has been hectic, yet January 2002 will always be defined by Jill and Jason's tragic car accident. Lord Jesus, I trust in your love for your children, I do not understand, yet I am sure of your love. You are God and I am not.

I made the journey to Beaumont on Sunday, I prayed a lot on the way down and then stood outside his door at St. Elizabeth's praying once again before I went in his room, because I suddenly felt a little nervous. I was greeted with a "Hey Bruce" from a bright eyed Jason; I was amazed he knew my name. His mom told him that "Bruce" was coming, so I don't know if he knew me or only knew that "Bruce" was coming. Soon after arriving in his room, ol' Bruce began to feel a bit dizzy, so I excused myself to the cafeteria and had a good lunch; then I felt just fine. Then after returning, Wendy, Audrey and I took Jason for a walk outside, the weather was beautiful, we walked, we dance, we sat in the grass. I picked a flower and handed it to Jason; he held it up to his nose (another victory in his mom's eyes—evidence of memory). After going back to the room, Jason was pretty tired. Jason's mom and I left Jason with Wendy and Audrey to say their goodbyes. Jason's mom and I talked out in the hall. She is amazing, energetic, focused and passionate in her love of God and her son. We talked about a prayer request for Jason: healthy enough (no fever) so he could go to the rehab center. After Audrey & Wendy left, Jason slept. His mom and I chatted in his room: 541. After a while she left me with Jason for an hour, and I read to him and spoke to him. He kept getting up and down. We finally went to the restroom: he's getting better at that, but we still needed to change clothes. It was pretty hard because he was either sleeping or getting up constantly. By faith I spoke God's word to Jason, reading him verses about Jesus opening the disciples' mind, Jer. 29:11, renewing your mind, Rom 12:2. Wendy and Audrey came back by because they had forgotten to take Jason's picture, so I was glad to get my picture taken with Jason. I hope I get a copy. I took my Mr. Buck teeth with me and tried to get Jason to laugh, everyone else did, but Jason didn't; I introduced myself as "Cousin Lester," cousin Lester got the brains, but I got the good looks. I would have to wait until later to get a laugh out of Jason. His rehab doctor came and asked Jason his name "Betty - Betty Smith"? We all laughed and wondered. Jason shook his hand, and identified 2 fingers, 3, 4, 5 - then the Dr. started pulling fingers down, but Jason kept counting up 6,7,8, we laughed again, I hope it didn't hurt Jason's feelings.

Lord Jesus, restore your servant Jason's mind. By faith I lift him up to you, by faith I open up the roof above and lower him on a mat to your feet Lord Jesus, I plead like the widow to hear my prayer, with the faith of the centurion - you say the word and it is done. Lord, I lift Jason up to you.

March 3, 2002, Sunday a.m.

Jason Mirikitani called me last week, Wednesday night. It blessed me, thrilled me. He is doing so much better, he remembers a lot but there are many things he has no memory of e.g. "Was I a good Dad"?!!? He will be coming to town next week (March 10) I am excited to be able to spend a little time with him. He really had become a good friend. I loved my time going around Lake Hefner on the tandem bike.

One time the back tire went flat, but we peddled on and finally made it. Oh the difference a little well placed air can make. It's the difference between walking in the flesh and walking in the Spirit, wouldn't you really rather walk in the power God intended for you rather than go through life on a flat tire? Lord Jesus fill me once again with Your Spirit, that I might live life in your power, not my own.

March 11, 2002, Monday a.m.

Well into March, the seasons are changing but not without a fight. Thank you Lord for this reminder that You are still in control. You are God and I am not. I find a lot of comfort in that.

Yesterday was a great day. The big highlight on miracle Sunday was seeing Jason Mirikitani preach at Britton Christian. It was amazing, when I saw him in Beaumont seven weeks ago, he thought his name was Betty Smith, and there, Jason was in the pulpit proclaiming Gods word! It was amazing. I was full of tears, not crying but with wet eyes witnessing a miracle. We watched Jason interact with the congregation afterwards, and it appeared that he had a lot of memories from each person. He was recalling a lot of details. I stood in awe of God's mercy and healing and was thankful for seeing Jason back in the saddle again.

December 30, 2002

Another year is about to pass into the "history" category. 2002 will always be defined by the Mirikitani family for me. Wow, the miracles in the midst of tragedy.

MILE

Sometimes You Can't Make It On Your Own
—Bono[28]

Mike Hays—Mike was my Oklahoma City pastor, and someone who I often looked to in that town as another spiritual big brother. His dear friendship to me passed the test when he quickly traveled to Texas to sit at my bedside and help me along on my first recovery walks. Mike will always hold a special place close to my heart.

March 31, 2002

Life can be like that you know? One day you are riding the waves of satisfaction when suddenly the waves begin to beat so fiercely upon the hull of your heart that it breaks into shreds. One day you are enjoying life to its full and the next day finds you looking into a mirror and seeing nothing but emptiness and sorrow. Have you ever ridden that roller coaster of emotion that I am speaking of this morning? I have a few friends who have taken the ride.

Just this past week Bobby Ross from the Daily Oklahoman sat in my office. He was writing a story about Jason and Jill Mirikitani and wanted to ask me some questions. As we talked I focused on January 13th and January 15th.

---

28 U2, *Sometimes You Can't Make It On Your Own—How to Dismantle an Atomic Bomb* (New York, NY: Island Records, 2004), CD.

January 13th was a "Kodak Moment" for Jason and Jill and all of our church. I was away that morning, preaching at Village Christian Church as they had lost their pastor and we were helping them with their loss.

Jill sang the most beautiful song before Jason ever stood to preach. She sang the Easter story of the two followers of Jesus who were walking away from Jerusalem with their heads down, dejected, and feeling all alone after Jesus' death. Before the end of Jill's song Jesus

By Mike Hays
(to Britton Christian Church)

joined the two men. As he took the bread their eyes were opened and their sorrow turned to exuberant joy...Jesus opened their eyes and they could see. Jill's countenance changed as she began to sing the chorus,

Yes, I can see who walks with me
I can see who speaks my name
And I can feel something stirring in my heart
How His words ring strong and true
Like a once familiar strain
And I know that I'll never be the same
I can see
I can see
I can see!

Following Jill's song, Jason preached for the very first time at our church and it was a sermon that struck a chord in so many hearts. God used Jason to drive home one of the most important biblical truths that you and I can cling to in life – When you can't see God's hand you can trust His heart. He repeated that phrase over and over again. He told stories from his own life to illustrate his sermon, as well as stories from the lives of men and women who are written about in God's Word. By the end of the sermon there was not a soul present who walked away wondering what God was trying to teach us.

I talked to Jason after he preached that day and he was so honored to have the opportunity to teach God's Word. Sunday, January 13th was a glorious moment for Jason and Jill. Just two days later their joy, and ours, turned to sorrow. Deep, agonizing sorrow, that is still with us today. We learned on January 15th that Jason and Jill had been in a car wreck, Jill had died, and Jason was not expected to live through the night. Oh, there were so many plans, such a promising future, the sky was the limit for the ministry that God had given to these two, young, talented friends of ours.

How can you experience such different emotions in the span of three days? How can you go from the thrill of joyous celebration to the depths of devastation in less than a week? We all asked the question...

| MILE |

**No matter how steep the mountain—
the Lord is going to climb it with you.
—Helen Steiner Rice**

Jan Mirikitani—It's hard to think of enough adjectives to describe my mother and all that she gave in my recovery process to ensure my well-being and restoration. She was selfless, sacrificial, giving, and faithful throughout my recovery. I love and appreciate my mom so much, and what I'm enclosing here below is a brief portion of a letter that she comprised just one month after the accident, that was then mailed out to folks who had committed to praying for me. As you read it, you'll see that she was exhorting our friends to keep the necessary faith in our trustworthy God as they prayed for my healing and restoration. My mom is really a "super-Sherpa," enduring weeks and weeks of nights with just a few hours of sleep, to ensure my well-being. Perhaps one of the strongest testimonies to the kindness of her character is that before I was re-potty-trained, I used the bathroom on her leg, and she nicely informed me how great that was, and how next time I should do that in a toilet! The Bible describes faith as "being sure of what you hope for and certain of what you do not see." (Hebrews 11:1) It seems pretty clear that Jan Mirikitani is a woman of faith, who, thankfully, raised her son in that same certainty in a trustworthy God.

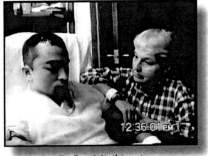

By Jan Mirikitani

(Feb. 22, 2002)

...the parted Red Sea, the falling walls of Jericho, the unsinged hair of the believers in the fiery furnace... Let us not be like the children of Israel, who over and over saw God's miracles, and then forgot about them... We know God will restore Jason completely to Himself, to Shiloh, to sweet Abigail...

MILE

"For I know the plans I have for you," declares the LORD,
"plans to prosper you and not to harm you,
plans to give you hope and a future."
Jeremiah 29:11 (NIV)

Painting Abby's Nails

Photo by Barb Raney

"To her the name of father was another name for love."
—Fanny Fern

"Children are like wet cement.
Whatever falls on them makes an impression."
—Dr. Haim Ginott

As a child I often put together model airplanes and cars. Sometimes, my dad joined me assembling these toys. He would painstakingly work with me to transform the small pieces of wood or plastic to more closely resemble the real things. Working side by side, we glued them together, carefully assembling the decals. And finally, we finished with my favorite step—the paint. With the precision of a surgeon, I would delicately slide the brush across the model, then sit back and admire my fine replica.

Little did I suspect that this talent I gained while growing up would later equip me in something equally as delicate, yet much more precious—painting Abby's nails.

Fully operating as "Mr. Mom" and, therefore, nail-painter-extraordinaire by the beginning of 2003, Abby and I moved back to our little house in Oklahoma City. I did my best to handle all of the parenting responsibilities, which included her nail care, brushing her hair with "detangler" (which, as I soon learned, didn't work nearly as well as simply washing her hair with shampoo and *conditioner*). Occasionally, I even forged into the uncertain territory of hair maintenance—namely cutting her bangs.

Besides various tangible responsibilities, I should revisit something here that I mentioned only briefly earlier. Abby was a precious child who had no memory of her mom, but all of her friends at daycare, church, and in the neighborhood had mothers. At her day care, all the other children were picked up by their mothers. I was certainly the only single dad there or in almost any social setting that we attended.

My sensitive spirit reminded me that Abby needed emotional stability, security, and happiness without any questions. Her tiny heart was so easily influenced at this stage that I couldn't afford to feel sorry for myself, to mope around, or be anything but cheerful.

This was extremely tough and unnatural for me given all that I was enduring. There were nights when I cried myself to sleep, and there were mornings when I woke up and wished it was all just a bad dream. So for Abby's sake especially, I often got on my knees and asked God for His joy to be my daily strength (Nehemiah 8:10). He, of course, faithfully provided and equipped as needed.

Like a lot of children, Abby spelled love T-I-M-E, which worked out well for us, because we had lots of that together. Shiloh hired me as its Executive Director, but raising my daughter came first on my priority list. At first, I worried that she had no mother, but I later took comfort in the fact that our heavenly Father would equip me with everything I needed. He faithfully provided a particular young lady at Abby's preschool who showed her extra special attention and care, filling an emotional gap in her little heart each day.

As for me, I decided to make the best out of the situation. From the beginning, I always felt it was my job to *make memories* with my child, and I knew that traditions helped make a child feel secure. When I put her to bed each night, I started a silly series of bed time rituals. These included my best verbal impression of Winnie the Pooh, a bedtime story from one of her children's Bibles, and three songs: "Twinkle, Twinkle, Little Star," "ABC's," and "Jesus Loves Me." Sometimes, I accompanied the songs with an instrument of sorts, like a "thumb piano" or an xylophone.

MILE

Children will not remember you for the material things you provided but for the feeling that you cherished them.
—Richard L. Evans

We had our necessary weekly trips to Super Wal-Mart, and during those treks, Abby knew that if she was helpful, I would buy her some kind of inexpensive toy or treat. Every Saturday morning, we had the tradition of both putting on our aprons and chef hats and making scrambled eggs and bacon together. I taught her how to crack the eggs, how to mix them up, and how to spread them around the skillet, while standing on her stool in front of the stove. All of that was almost as fun as dressing the part in our chef outfits. It's hard to say who looked forward to Saturday mornings more.

While I may have received an E for effort those days, and I sincerely did my best to make it clear to Abby that her daddy treasured her, I should admit that I took one or two "fatherly" shortcuts since there was no mother around and I didn't have to answer to a wife. For instance, almost every night, I dressed Abby in her outfit for the next day, instead of in her pajamas. This allowed me to cut corners a bit on the getting ready process the next day. As silly as that may sound, Abby's heart trusted that my love for her wasn't going anywhere, and that she was the most important person in my life.

As a single father, I did do a few extras for Abby though, that don't cause my friends to laugh at me, but rather to pat me on the back. For instance, I occasionally pulled out the extra sewing machine that my mother gave me and applied the skills I'd learned in my 8th grade home economics class (memories that were surprisingly still intact despite my brain injury), and I would make Abby pillowcases. And these pillowcases were amazing, in my humble opinion. Not to sound arrogant, because I realize pillowcases are an extremely simple craft, but Abby looked forward to laying her head down at night on her special pillows. For they were really a reflection of her father's love and care for her.

MILE

**"Fatherhood is pretending the present
you love most is soap-on-a-rope."
—Bill Cosby**

One afternoon, before her bedtime, I reached for a pill, to take my pain medicine. Abby was three or four years old and she noted, "Daddy's taking his medicine."

I replied, "Yep, from when I hurt my head and neck in the car accident."

Abby then said, "I know, I remember."

I thought, *"Sure, you remember."*

Abby was only 15 months old the day of the accident and no one had ever told her what happened that day. She had bare bone details to give her an understanding of why I went through all I did.

So I decided to dig a little deeper. "What do you remember, kiddo?" I asked.

She answered, "They took you away for a while in a copler," and I was sad" (in Abby-terms at that age, "a copler" meant a helicopter).

To that response, I nearly collapsed. When I gathered my thoughts and emotions, I faintly replied, "Do you remember anything else, Abby?"

"Yes," she said. "They brought you back after a while, and I was happy."

At this, I cried. I smiled. I hugged her, and I thanked God for her sweet child's heart and for giving us that brief but poignant interaction.

My work at Shiloh was another blessing in Abby's young life. At her fingertips were horses to ride, a pond in which to fish, and a zip-line to ride while nestled snugly to my back. I'm so thankful for the time God provided Abby and me in those days, especially on the Shiloh camp grounds. For example, we would occasionally camp out at night near our small pond, without really "roughing it" at all. Instead, I would bring a small pizza for us to share, along with a portable DVD player and one of her favorite movies—we would enjoy *all* of those things inside the tent. After we'd caught a few small fish with canned corn as bait, we would eat the pizza, use the restroom in our office, and then go to sleep.

If it was a rainy night, we did everything the same minus the fishing and the tent. In place of the tent, Abby and I would actually sleep in my car, a Honda Element, which has seats that mount up, leaving a large flat area for us to spread out our sleeping bags and pillows. Since the car has a moon roof too, we especially *liked* rainy campouts.

Abby loved all of our campouts, and I was glad to make fun memories with my child. Since I was Shiloh's director, we had a wooded area and a fishing pond readily accessible.

**"Any man can be a father.
It takes someone special to be a dad."
—Author Unknown**

My work at Shiloh included long days preparing to launch and run this new youth camp ministry. While I did this, Abby attended a local daycare. In the evening, after I picked her up, we would play, eat, and take part in our bedtime rituals. After she went to bed, I either pulled my laptop back out to do more Shiloh work, or I talked on the phone, watched a movie, or played video games.

However, my heart still ached, as I felt sad and lonely. I could not act as if *everything* had suddenly become perfect inside of me, simply because my daughter and I had such a wonderful relationship. The house became dreadfully quiet by 9:00 every night. To the point that I watched every movie that I'd ever owned, just to avoid the painful noiselessness. Some nights were better than others, and every night, of course, I would eventually grow weary, and doze off to sleep.

I realized that without a doubt, I needed to continue to make sure that I grieved the loss of Jill properly. I had a friend who could help me along that path, as a licensed Christian Counselor in Oklahoma City. We began meeting on a weekly basis with the intended purpose of helping me along in my mourning process. My friend led me through the difficult "time to mourn" (Ecclesiastes 3:4), so that I could come out the backside with sweet memories that I could more easily embrace, and eventually share with Abby. After meeting with him for several months, I felt assured that, although I had endured some severe emotional wounding along with my physical injuries, I could now readily move forward without hesitation.

I should emphasize *without hesitation*, because sometimes I wished that the "move forward" didn't seem so slow. Throughout all of Scripture, from Genesis to Revelation, the most often asked inquiry is, "How long, O Lord, how long?"[29] It seems that the people of God consistently cried out for relief, which were the cries of my heart at this time. Ironically, though, the most repeated command from God is "Do not

---

29   Psalm 6:3, 13:1-2, 35:17, 79:5, 80:4, 82:2, 89:46, 90:13, 94:3, 119:84; Isaiah 6:11; Jer. 12:4; Hab. 1:2, 2:6; Zech. 1:12; Rev. 6:10.

fear" or "Do not be afraid."[30] God does not give a direct answer to the "How long?" question. Instead, he responds with His own imperative which, in essence says, "Trust me. I've got everything under control."

I recently came across a real life application of these Scriptures at the time of this writing that blew me away. One of my seminary professors was down in Haiti and spoke about a man he met whose house was destroyed in a recent hurricane. This man would be forced now to live in a church with 150 others. I thought of all that man had lost and would now be forced to deal with, not to mention his loss of privacy, and having to wait in line just to simply use the restroom!

My friend asked the man, "*How long* will this problem last?"

The Haitian man quickly replied, "I don't know. But God does. And He can be trusted."

My eyes got wet as I heard these words... I couldn't help but question myself and my own (lack of) faith. I don't easily trust God in the midst of such obvious trials. I then realized that throughout Scripture, it was trials that *led* people to a place of more complete reliance and dependence upon God. And it was there that they learned He was trustworthy. I was both encouraged and challenged by this man who had hope in spite of the hurricane.

In my own situation, I'll admit that God showed His kindness to me by responding to *my* "How long?" question in like form with numerous calls to trust His gracious nature, but my severely shaken faith in Him needed to be restored. This

---

30   Gen. 15:1, 21:17, 26:24, 46:3; Ex. 14:13; Num. 21:34; Deut. 1:17, 1:21, 1:29, 3:2, 3:22, 7:18, 18:22, 20:1, 31:6; Josh. 8:1, 10:8, 10:25, 11:6; Jud. 6:23; 1 Sam. 12:20; 2 Kings 1:15, 19:6; 1 Chron. 22:13, 28:20; 2 Chron. 20:15, 20:17, 32:7; Isaiah 10:24, 37:6, 40:9, 41:14, 43:5, 44:2, 44:8, 54:4; Jer. 1:8, 42:11; Ezekiel 2:6, 3:9; Dan. 10:12, 10:19; Zech. 8:13, 8:15; Mt. 1:20, 10:26, 10:28, 28:5, 28:10; Lk. 1:13, 1:30, 2:10, 12:4, 12:32; Jn. 12:15 (Zech. 9:9), 14:27; Acts 18:9, 27:24; Rev. 1:17, 2:10

would soon begin to take place, as I was starting to understand the meaning of dependable Fatherhood myself.

MILE

**"Father!—to God himself we cannot give a holier name.
William Wordsworth**

Recently, I let Abby, who is now ten years old, read the last part of this chapter. She was shocked to learn of the grief and discouragement that I felt at this time, how I sought emotional relief. She had no previous awareness of these matters as I had kept them hidden from her. After these revelations, she was both amazed and thankful that she'd only seen happiness in her daddy's countenance.

Christe

Christe Boen

"Love comforteth like sunshine after the rain." [31]
—William Shakespeare

**"Being deeply loved by someone gives you strength,
while loving someone deeply gives you courage."**
—Lao Tzu

I initially intended to call this chapter, "A New Beginning," or "A God-Send," but as I thought about it, I chose instead to name it after the woman who *God sent* to be my *new beginning*: Christe. My original chapter titles were something of a misnomer. They perhaps described the

---

31   William Shakespeare, *Venus and Adonis*, 799—804.

situation I was in, but they didn't capture the person that I met, fell in love with, and with whom I experienced a deeper healing. This chapter is the rest of the story.

Being widowed left me with a great sense of loss and loneliness. I experienced these feelings emotionally, mentally, physically, and practically. There were daily reminders like the empty chair at the dinner table, no one to hug and kiss me when I came home at night, and the empty side of my bed (until I bought the twin). This began to leave a dry taste in my mouth, and regularly remind me of my heartfelt desire and need for a bride.

In fact, one day, during an unplanned lunch shortly after summer camp in 2004, I expressed some of these feelings to my good friend Pastor Mike. Since Mike Hays was my pastor besides a Shiloh Board Member, I often spoke to him about personal stuff. Moreover, I told Mike that my life was majorly unbalanced, that all I did was Shiloh and Abby.

Looking back, I realize I was speaking out of emotional fatigue. I'm glad that Mike was supportive of my lunchtime decision (that shocked many others) to resign as Shiloh's Executive Director. Also, he agreed with my decision to move back to St. Louis where my parents would provide my life with balance and lots of help with Abby. This seemed like the clearest and most sensible decision, when I really took an honest look at my situation.

So I discussed the matter with Abby, and after talking through a few questions, my four year old daughter and I agreed on this decision that evening. She was especially excited about the opportunity to see my parents, Mawmaw and Pawpaw, more often, of course. It was not long after our move back to St. Louis that Abby and I were able to move into our own place not too far from their home. I was able to quickly find a job, using my college business degree, with my brother who is a local financial planner. So, thankfully, because of my faithful family and God's grace, I had a home and a source of income after our move back to St. Louis.

Interestingly, it also wasn't long before my friend, Dale, was ready to "set me up" with a girl he knew. He told me I had to meet Christe Boen. "She's very pretty," he said, "and she is a strong Christian." He went on to explain that she also had many connections with the St. Louis Cardinals due to the fact that her mom started the "Christian Family Day" program at Busch Stadium. Because I trusted my friend and he genuinely seemed to think we'd be a good fit, I agreed to meet her and asked him to arrange a low-pressure way to make that happen. Obviously, this was a set-up, and Dale was playing "match-maker," neither of which I was too comfortable with in my early 30's.

MILE

"When I was nine, I had this girlfriend and we used to have running races in the park. I wanted to be like Superman and fly in and rescue her."
—Orlando Bloom

So my friend invited Christe to come over that night and help us as we stuffed envelopes for a ministry fundraiser. When I saw her, my immediate thought was to correct Dale because his description didn't do her justice at all! She was *gorgeous*, but I had to focus on staying cool and relaxed. I could feel my pulse quickening in my chest.

It turns out that Christe had recently seen me on TV when a local cable station featured my accident and recovery.

"Are you still in pain?" she asked.

"Yes," I answered.

So she dug in her purse, found one of her chiropractic business cards, and told me, "I think I can help you out."

Honestly doubtful, I wasn't sure there was much she could do to help me. But she was so sweet and compassionate, and I could tell she really wanted to try. I figured why not. *Even if my neck was still sore, my eyes wouldn't be sore at all!* So, of course, as a sensible man, I took her card, expressed my thanks, tried to stop myself from stammering, and called her the next morning to set up my first appointment.

At that time, my medical doctors had given me a pain reliever that I was taking four times daily. The phrase "pain in the neck" was all too familiar to me, as I lived with it as a literal part of my life, given that neck pain always resurfaced every three to four hours, usually feeling like a mild soreness. Since the medicine seemed to offer no hope of permanent elimination of this aching pain, I honestly thought that I was destined to take these pills for the rest of my life.

However, on my first visit to see Christe, she explained more about chiropractic procedures and her hopes and intentions for her patients of wellness and improvement. She told me, "We feel in chiropractic medicine that the body is able to heal itself, but that sometimes we need to give it a jumpstart."

That made a lot of sense to me, and, although I was pessimistic about any results, I was certainly willing to give it a shot, even though I lacked *faith*, which Phillip Yancey says, "means believing in advance what will only make sense in reverse."[32] After all, according to Scripture,

---

32   Philip Yancey, *Disappointment With God* (Grand Rapids, MI: Zondervan, 1997), 224.

> Faith is being sure of what we hope for and certain of what
> we do not see.
>
> Hebrews 11:1 (NIV)

While some people may refer to that as stupid "blind faith," it is what I've based most practical decisions in my life upon as a Christian, since I was raised to "fix my eyes not on what is seen, but on what is unseen," (2 Cor. 4:18) a standard which has always proven reliable to me.

I wish I would have possessed such faith in this particular instance, because in just a month, which included weekly adjustments and occasional acupuncture, my pain decreased enough that I actually needed one less pill each day! Instead of taking four pills, every 3-4 hours, I was taking only three. After another month, that number reduced again down to two, until by the end of four months, with the help of my new chiropractor friend, *I was completely off my meds,* and I was overjoyed, amazed, and thrilled. "All I have needed (God's) hand hath provided."[33] His grace is truly sufficient (2 Cor. 12:9).

MILE

**"Love cures people—both the ones who give it
and the ones who receive it."
—Karl Menninger**

Equally healing to my well-being was the fact that with each appointment and adjustment, I got to know Christe a little bit better. Looking back, *I now realize that I was receiving both physical and emotional healing simultaneously,*

---

33 Words: Thomas Chisholm, Music: William Runyan, *Great Is Thy Faithfulness* (1923).

which literally makes sense, since the Bible tells us, "A joyful heart is good medicine" (Prov. 17:22a, ESV). Yes, my neck and head were receiving weekly chiropractic adjustments, but my heart was also accepting some regular healing treatments in terms of simply feeling upbeat, blessed, and happy instead of weighty and downtrodden. For the first time in a long time, I looked forward to seeing a certain pretty lady on a weekly basis.

Given the fact that I was so attracted to Christe, I began to concoct random reasons to call her each week. I only had her office number so I would call with my aimless question just so I could hear her voice. One week, after I'd called on a Thursday, she returned my call on her *cell phone.* She later told me that she was intentionally giving me half-a-chance, since the motives behind my random, weekly calls were becoming pretty obvious. By returning my call on her cell phone, I now possessed her personal contact number. This was a major score in my book.

My excitement over having her number increased even more when I called her back and learned that she was driving to her alma mater, the University of Missouri, for a chiropractic conference. This was an amazing coincidence as I too was headed to Columbia with the college wrestling team that I helped coach with my dad. I explained this to Christe, and asked her if she could take me (and another assistant coach) out for a late dinner after her conference. To my delight, she said she'd be glad to. After we got off the phone, I was thankful I didn't have time to think or plan that one out, because I think I would have messed it up. But, of course, I wanted us to be able to hang out socially, outside of her chiropractic office, and now that was beginning.

Lord knows that I was a lonely man who desperately wanted to find a wife. But prior to meeting Christe, every time I became interested in dating someone, I felt as if God would *check* my spirit, and tell me to keep my focus solely on raising Abby. So I would return 100% attention in that fatherhood direction. However, from my first meeting with Christe forward, I never once felt that kind of hesitation, only complete freedom that she was a safe person to pursue.

Remember this picture of our first meeting scene. Seated is a widower who has been raising a daugher alone for 4½ years, and in walks a blonde haired, blue eyed beauty with a compassionate, kind heart, an intelligent, scholarly, medical mind, and even an all-American level athleticism (Christe was a softball pitcher at Mizzou on a four year scholarship). I honestly felt terrified that, within seconds, I would feel that old check in my spirit. Instead, I was delighted to find that all those checks had simply been there for the Lord to remind me to focus initially and completely on Abby in some key stages in her early life, while holding out as He prepared me for the perfect partner whom he had also been readying. Now what lay ahead was sweet romance.

When her chiropractic program ended that night, Christe came by our hotel, and we all headed out for pizza together at Shakespeare's©, a local college hang-out. It was the perfect atmosphere to mark our first social time together. That pizza dinner set the pace for us to begin spending time together in similar fashions thereafter, getting to know each other better personally. Neither of us could have guessed that a conversation at Shakespeare's Pizza© would be the starting point of such a lasting and sweet relationship. We randomly talked about the movie, "The Princess Bride," at one point in conversation, and she admitted she had never seen it. I gladly took this as my cue to invite her over for a movie night the next week at my house. I even offered to cook her dinner—teriyaki chicken and rice.

Admittedly, I was a bit nervous before this evening, being in my early 30's back in the dating game. But honestly only just a little nervous, as I sincerely felt a lot of peace about this connection with Christe, and it seemed like God was in the center of drawing us together. All I told Abby was that the nice lady that she met the week earlier was going to come over, and that we were going to watch that fun "Princess Bride" movie together. Abby didn't think anything of it that she showed. She was just excited about me cooking teriyaki and rice and us watching, "The Princess Bride."

Christe's perception of the situation, and specifically of me, was transitioning, though, triggered by that evening's events. While watching me with Abby and eating a tasty home-cooked meal, Christe thought of me as both a great father, and a great cook. Admittedly, I lucked into both of those assessments. I'd been marinating the chicken teriyaki for a day and a half; so it was extra flavorful. And I'd been a solo parent for a few years by this point; I'd had lots of dad-practice. Christe admits now that she initially thought I was cute when she saw me on TV, and especially liked that I was wearing a Christian t-shirt. I would later find out that occurrences like these would add fuel to my attraction fire in her heart.

Another bonus that helped me that night was small but meaningful. I enjoy giving people unique and special gifts, and I knew that Christe was enthralled by Paris. So I found her a small brass Eiffel Tower pencil sharpener that luckily arrived in the mail that same night when she came over. As a matter of fact, this little pencil sharpener began a trend of my giving her some kind of gift, big or small, every single time I was with her, an action I realized meant a lot to her, as it showed her the thoughts of my heart. I know that some people think of gift-giving as a shallow activity, but I hoped that instead it showed her that I thought a lot about her, even when we weren't together.

I also made a mental note that Christe enjoyed spending uninterrupted quality time with friends, just talking and relaxing. So as a second gift, I intentionally shopped for an Eiffel Tower puzzle for us to work on together while just sitting and talking. I found it online too, and I had it rush-shipped to my house so that I could have her over that next week with something fun for us to do after dinner.

After numerous evenings together like this, we ended up, unintentionally, having a very honest and serious talk, with fantastic results. Towards the end, we agreed that we both wanted to only date each other. As we closed this conversation, that was initially scary to me, Christe looked at me and said:

"Since we're exclusive now, I'll need to tell a few other guys to stop calling me."

I was so glad, that I just said something like, "Yep!"

Part of that conversation included one of my most fearful realities:

I asked, "Are you at all concerned about me having a child?"

I was somewhat terrified to ask this question. On the other hand, I realized there was no point in pursuing a dating relationship with a woman who would not embrace my daughter. In this moment, my faith was really put to the test.

She expressed that she felt terrible for me that I had been widowed, but that Abby was simply a "bonus in our relationship." Feeling elated and relieved, I climbed into my twin bed that night, and the classic Shakespearian line floated through my head:

"Good night, good night! Parting is such sweet sorrow,
That I shall say good night till it be morrow."[34]

---

34   William Shakespeare, *Romeo and Juliet* II, ii, 176—185.

Perhaps it was no accident that our first social outing had been at *Shakespeare's* Pizza.©

I appreciate and enjoy so many things about Christe, in addition to the initial attraction I felt. But something that I specifically grew to love about her was her kind, gracious, and compassionate spirit. Christe always tries to help people who need a hand or who are hurting in some way. In fact, that is one of the main reasons that she decided to pursue a career in chiropractic medicine, because she specifically wanted to help others in effective ways that she knew would work. As a reputable chiropractic doctor now, countless patients love coming to Dr. Boen, who adjusts them as an excellent chiropractor and listens to them like a caring counselor.

MILE

"Love is the greatest refreshment in life."
—Pablo Picasso

Albert Einstein once said, "Gravitation cannot be held responsible for people falling in love." For the first time in several years, I sensed that I might be falling in love again, and perhaps draw this beautiful woman's heart to the new me. I sure wanted to fall in love again, and I was already starting to think that I wanted this woman to fall in love with me!

In retrospect, when I first met Christe Boen, I thought she was very sweet and attractive. She extended such kindness and hope to all of her patients and friends who were hurting both physically and emotionally, because her heart was so full of love and grace. These traits were especially appealing to me because of my past, and I was thrilled that she seemed to like me too. I wasn't too bothered by the fact that she was about an inch and a half taller than me.

MILE

**You have captured my heart, my treasure, my bride.
You hold it hostage with one glance of your eyes.
Song of Solomon 4:9a (NLT)**

Abby, like a lot of little girls, loved the Disney Princesses, and so she once asked me what a stepmother was. I told her that they aren't *always* evil, like in those fairytales. "If I were to get married again," I told her, "that woman would be your stepmother." Looking in my daughter's eyes, I promised that I would never marry anyone unless Abby shared a love for that woman. I'll never forget the grin that spread across her little face. "Okay," she replied, and together we moved forward.

Christe was extremely tender and kindhearted towards Abby. She took the sweet initiative to spend Tuesday after-school times with her as a traditional "play-day." This became a new tradition that Abby loved. Christe and Abby fell into a relationship with one another, greatly enjoying each other's company, and Christe began to undergo a maternal metamorphosis in my eyes during these weekly "play-days" with my daughter. While Abby never talked a lot about the specifics of those days, she always made it clear how much fun she had with Christe, and how she looked forward to their next Tuesday together. It wasn't too long before Abby felt the same deep love for Christe as I did, and asked me if she could start calling her, "Mommy." That was all the confirmation I needed. I bought a ring one month later.

Being a hopeless romantic, I wanted to propose marriage to Christe in a sweet and meaningful way. Besides, I understand that ladies often ask each other about the proposal. And I wanted my special girl to have some serious bragging rights.

I had the idea to track down my favorite children's book from when I was growing up: Stop That Ball.[35] I did this very intentionally.

Stop That Ball is the story of a little boy enjoying an afternoon at play with his tethered big red ball. As happens any time a child is at play, something goes wrong that leads to a great and wonderful adventure. The string breaks, the ball gets loose, and the little boy follows it through the town in an effort to retrieve it. After a number of exciting events, it is finally blasted through the sky and lands in his own backyard. He arrives home to find that *someone* has already re-tethered it, so he immediately resumes an afternoon of play with his big red ball.

There is a certain little girl that appears almost hidden on nearly every page, and is once again present when the little boy arrives home to find his ball mysteriously tethered, indicating that perhaps she tethered it for him. I chose to read this book to Christe because she had been there so regularly in my life, just like the smiling little girl, helping me along in ways that at times I'm sure I wasn't even aware of. I explained all these things, right before her cell phone message alert rang.

I text messaged Christe sometimes, and always started off with her initials, "CB…" Before this night, I had preset a text that said, "CB, I would like for you to become CM." As she reached for her phone, read that, and then turned around to

---

35   Mike McClintock, *Stop That Ball* (New York, NY: Random House Children's Books, 1959)

me, I was waiting for her on my knee with the engagement ring in hand.

She said yes.

"A happy man marries the girl he loves;
A happier man loves the girl he marries."
—Anonymous

Reflecting on my years as "Mr. Mom," during which time I did my best to meet the needs of my child, I realized that Abby never once complained about the absence of a mommy. I have to think that every little girl at age 3 or 4 loves to talk about her mom. I also know, however, that God provided some wonderful female caregivers and loving people at her daycare and at our church during that difficult period, to make up for all the love that my own mother and aunt poured into Abby's heart during my injury recovery year of 2002.

Even though she was extremely young, Abby's perspective on all that went on, from the death of her birthmother, to being raised by only me, to my marriage to Christe, can be clearly and beautifully seen in some of her drawings that I treasure:

Abby & Daddy, December 2005

Daddy, Abby, Mommy, family dogs, April 2006

This chapter would be incomplete without mention of our newest blessing, our son, Josiah, whom Christe gave birth to in July, 2007. I know I'm a biased dad, but JoJo is about as sweet and cute as a little boy could ever be. He is adorable, smiles all the time, hugs frequently, and loves to play with me. He especially likes to act like David, with me as Goliath, so he can put his foot on my chest, pump his fist in the air, and shout, "Our God!" Christe is an amazing mom to him, and Abby is a super big sister.

Here's another one of Abby's drawings from last fall:

Abby's family drawing, September, 2007

You can see now why I initially thought of calling this chapter, "A God-Send," since the Lord graced me with love that I could not have deserved, and pain relief, both physically and emotionally through the help of Christe, not to mention that He sent Abby an unbelievable loving mother in the process. On top of all that, He also gave us a precious new baby boy.

Josiah in August, 2008
www.inthebeginningphoto.com

**"He who finds a wife finds what is good and
receives favor from the LORD."
Proverbs 18:22 (NIV)**

Paul told the Colossians, "He (Jesus) is before all things, and in him all things hold together." I was blessed to be living out that Scripture, as a living witness of one God had held together who had been falling apart physically, emotionally, and spiritually. But by God's grace and might, I was being restored.

He brought a beautiful and caring bride into my life who was also a fun and involved mother in Abby's. What a perfect fit for us both by the One who "holds all things together."

No wonder Jesus said, "My Father is always at His work to this very day, and I, too, am working" (John 5:17, NIV). I am thankful that He had been working continually on behalf of me and Abby since January of 2002.

MILE

"The love of a family is life's greatest blessing."
—Author Unknown

Incidentally, we have since been to the courthouse for our adoption docket (12/5/07), in order for Christe to become Abby's official adopted mother, a process that Jill's parents embraced as well. Also, we talk to and/or email Jill's parents weekly, and Abby sees them a few times each year. She especially loves visiting and helping out at their Texas ranch.

From Christe:

Almost 5 years ago, God put in my path an adorable man named Jason and his sweet daughter, Abby. Jason swept me off my feet almost immediately with his winsome smile and passion for the Lord. When Jason told me of his accident and head pain, I searched in my purse for a business card hoping I could help him but really thinking he was so cute I wanted to get to know him better. When I say Jason swept me off my feet, that is no exaggeration. I've never met a man that made me feel so special and important to him. It was evident to me that Jason was in a different place than any man I'd ever met before. He didn't want to miss any opportunity to express his love for me every time we were together. His regular gifts told me he was thinking of me often and that he listened to what I said was important to me. It was clear he held close the fact that tomorrow isn't promised to any of us. I felt grateful to be the recipient of this changed man and his new outlook.

Abby stole my heart right from the start. I can still picture her running to my car to greet me with a hug when I first came to their house to spend time with Jason. I never saw Abby as a red flag. I never imagined myself marrying a man with a child but I think God was preparing me for it my whole life. I have only had one other job besides a chiropractor and that is as a baby sitter. I love kids and Abby was very easy to love. Watching Jason and Abby interact sealed the deal for me. The relationship I witnessed between them inspired me. I knew I wanted this man to be the father to any future children we could have together. I saw how he gently molded her little heart to love Jesus. She has such a sensitive spirit to the things of God that could only come from her daddy pouring truth into her soul. I've since adopted Abby and

God has bonded our hearts together perfectly as mother and daughter. Abby is an amazing big sister to her little brother, Josiah. I feel so blessed to have her as a role model for him.

$$\boxed{\text{MILE}}$$

"I love the Lord because He hears and answers my prayers. Because He bends down and listens, I will pray as long as I have breath."
Psalm 116:1-2 (NLT)

My Delight[36]
Song (words & music) by Jason Mirikitani, January 2008

Once a man had a delight,
And though she was quite small,
To him she was so sweet and dear
That to her he gave his all.

So in her little heart and soul
He focused all his time,
And loving, faithful, Immanuel
Equipped his one-tracked mind.

But then one day God turned his eyes
To see a pretty treat
They met, they talked, and soon he saw
This one was also sweet!

---

36   See Appendix for "My Delight" children's book with illustrations.

And she was smart too, he learned,
She was exactly right.
Before he knew it, the man had found
A completely new delight.

The little one loved her too, of course,
And soon there came along
In all their lives a new delight
To make them four smiles strong!

BRIDGE:
Now the man has three delights,
And they are four smiles strong! (2x)

Abby's Song

Abby doing sign language to "How Great Is Our God"[37]

**"Those who sow in tears will reap with songs of joy."
Psalm 126:5 (NIV)**

"Fear ends where faith begins."[38]

---

37 Chris Tomlin, *How Great Is Our God—Arriving* (Franklin, TN: Six Step Records, 2004), CD.

38 7/20/05, Copyright © 2001 Georgio Dano, "This quote, I quoted in the Toronto Star during the 2002 World Youth Day, Toronto, Canada. It is referring to the fear of terrorism and the 1 million youth gathered to greet Pope John Paul II." (www.motivateus.com/cibt-51.htm)

In 1859, there was a stunt performer, or "daredevil," named Jean Francois Gravelet, who was known as "The Great Blondin," who became the first person to walk the 335 meters across Niagara Falls. Ever the showman, he performed this walk several different times, adding variety by doing different tricks on the tightrope, like walking across it blindfolded, or carrying his manager on his back while balancing on stilts. He once cooked and ate an omelet in the center of the rope.

On one occasion, he asked the crowd, "How many of you believe that I, 'The Great Blondin,' can walk across this tightrope to the other side?" Of course, his spectators responded wildly in the affirmative. So he walked across the tightrope and came back again. Then he asked them, "How many of you believe that I, 'The Great Blondin,' can not only walk back across that tightrope, but this time do it while I push a wheelbarrow?"

Again, the crowd assented, but one man, a little more enthusiastic than the others, caught "The Great Blondin's" eye. What really only lasted five seconds probably felt like about 5 minutes to this man, as his heart wrestled with the question of sincere trust, now that his eyes locked with a man who might soon be holding his very life in his hands. Suddenly, the reality of hopping into that wheelbarrow threatened his faith. Next, "The Great Blondin" pointed right at him and said, "If you really believe, then get in the wheelbarrow." The man quickly disappeared.

As a Christian, Jesus wants me to get into His wheelbarrow. That wheelbarrow represents what God wants to do that is unique in my life. Frankly, that's really scary. If there was no risk or uncertainty involved, I guess it wouldn't be called faith. The difference between what we say we believe and what we *really* believe will always show up in our actions. Jesus hears us say that we believe He can do anything He says, but if we aren't willing to get in the wheelbarrow, do we really believe?

"Faith sees the invisible, believes the unbelievable, and receives the impossible."
—Corrie ten Boom,
Nazi Concentration Camp Survivor, Author

Admittedly, my faith was severely jarred in January of 2002. Even though God Himself had been actively renewing and restoring my substantially shaken beliefs in His goodness, kindness, and grace in both my personal life and relationships, my outlook and perspective still occasionally wavered. I had once been gladly riding in His spiritual wheelbarrow, and now I had to decide whether or not I was willing to climb back in. This truly called into question my opinions about the Lord, His character and His workings, considerations that I'd had since an early age. Was He trustworthy in my personal life?

I certainly believed that God helped Biblical heroes out of jams, since I had heard stories like "Daniel in the Lions' Den," "Shadrach, Meshach, and Abednego," and "David and Goliath" since I was a child. However, it's an entirely different matter when *you* are the person in the fiery furnace, the lions' den, or on the battle field facing the giant. In my case, I realized that I was a lot like one of those characters for whom our God had a redeeming story after a horrible start. And I agreed with the wise man's words:

> *The end of a matter is better than its beginning.*
> Ecclesiastes 7:8a (NIV)

Yes, I had a substantial list of heartbreaking losses, things that shake a person's soul. People hope to never have to endure *any* such things, and I had to cope with *all* of them. However, God in His grace not only placed the right people in the exact perfect places at the correct times to rescue me from certain death, but He also restored me to health, and I was beginning to realize that He was now in the process of completely refreshing my spirit. So my faith was growing back up again.

In Mark's gospel, there is an account of a man whose son was possessed by an evil spirit. This man had enough faith to bring his son to Jesus as a solution, for help and deliverance, but when he encountered Jesus, he proclaimed, "*If* you can do anything, take pity on us and help us." To which Jesus responded, "'If you can'? Everything is possible to him who believes."

"Immediately the boy's father exclaimed, 'I do believe; help me overcome my unbelief!'" (Mark 9:22-24). Oh how I could relate to this unnamed man who so loved his son, who had just a little bit of faith and wanted Jesus to grace him with more faith along with the restoring act. Of course, Jesus freely gave him a dose of faith and then "rebuked the evil spirit," helping the boy to his feet (Mark 9:26-27). Honestly, where else could we go with our doubts and fears but to the gracious "Father of compassion and God of all comfort" (2 Cor. 1:3)?

New Testament *faith* like this comes from a Greek word [pisteuo] that means having far more than only mental ascent. Pisteuo, rather, is a full, overwhelming sense of trust, belief, and confidence, a persuasion that something is definitely true. We can all understand this practically because we ride elevators trusting designers, we cross bridges trusting builders, we sit on chairs trusting carpenters, and we eat at restaurants trusting chefs. At the youth camps I'd worked at, I'd even put faith in my ropes course equipment before going up forty feet in the air on the wires in the tops of trees. Accordingly, this is the Biblical definition of faith that I was relearning:

Now faith is being sure of what we hope for and certain of what we do not see.
Hebrews 11:1 (NIV)

So my accident recovery was not only physical and emotional; it was also *spiritual.*

MILE

"Faith is like electricity. You can't see it, but you can see the light."
—Author unknown

An inspirational movie recently came out that tells the true story of an eight year old boy going through a major trial. As a response to the suggestions to "pray," he decided to write a letter to God. He began to write Him a letter almost every day, talking to Him like He was a friend who cared and could help. He then began to develop an amazing sense of peace to which others were drawn, and he saw answers to his "prayers." His confidence grew and everyone around him was affected by his trusting demeanor. Lives were changed because this little guy decided to talk to God in a sincere believing way.[39]

While I did not write "Letters to God"[40] my faith in Him and my relationship with Him was certainly changing for the better, as like the boy in the movie, I was beginning to see the Lord as a friend who cared and could help.

MILE

"The LORD is my strength and my song."
Exodus 15:2, Psalm 118:14, Isaiah 12:2

God also used my sweet little daughter, Abigail, to strengthen my faith. Actually, the two examples that I'm going to mention here both involve the hit Christian song by Chris Tomlin, "How Great Is Our God,"[41] which means more to me now that I more accurately *understand* God's greatness. I rarely make it through the entirety of that song with dry eyes, knowing personally the truth that its words express over and over.

Whenever I mow the grass, I listen to my iPod©, and I occasionally sing along with whatever song is playing. One time, "How Great Is Our God"[42] streamed through; so I gladly sang along. Meanwhile, Abby was out on the patio playing and heard me. Having learned the signs to this particular song at her Christian school, I looked over to see her *doing the sign*

---

39   Thoughts from a devotional by Lorenzo and Jennifer Dunford, www.dunfordfamilyministries.com.
40   *Letters to God.* Possibility Pictures, 2010.
41   Chris Tomlin, *How Great Is Our God—Arriving* (Franklin, TN: Six Step Records, 2004), CD.
42   Ibid.

language along with my words to the song. I noticed this at the end of the chorus, and I paused my iPod© to wave at her. She encouraged me to keep singing because she wanted to keep signing with the song. So I hit the play button and continued, this time with watery eyes.

I shouldn't have been surprised then at the following occurrence. A few weeks later, Christe, Abby, and I went out to dinner at a local Mexican restaurant, and they had a singer off to the side with his guitar, offering live music during dinner. Abby asked me if she could have a quarter to give the man a tip. I found one in my pocket, and we went up to him together. He kindly offered to play a song of her choosing, asking if she had any favorites. Abby responded, "Well, I like 'How Great Is Our God.'"[43] He smiled and told her that he wasn't familiar with that tune. She replied, "That's okay. Thanks though." I smiled as we walked back to our seats together, holding the hand of a little girl who, without hesitation, asked the restaurant singer to play a song about her God's greatness and splendor.

In a secular world, it thrills my heart to know that our young daughter still has a pure heart, and that she already delights in the one who "stands age to age," with "time in His hands."

"How great is our God."[44]

MILE

"Faith is a bird that feels dawn breaking and sings while it is still dark."
—Scandinavian Saying

---

43   Ibid.
44   Ibid.

Powerful Weakness

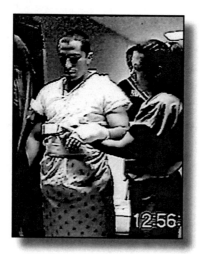

"Yeah, well, sometimes nothin' can be a real cool hand."
—Lucas Jackson ("Cool Hand Luke")

"God created the world out of nothing, and as long as we are nothing, He can make something out of us."
—Martin Luther

The Apostle Paul wrote roughly half of the entire New Testament, but before he became a tremendous missionary, Paul was known as a killer. He took part in the slaying of many 1st Century Christians. As you would guess, a substantial metamorphosis and transformation occurred in the heart and mind of this man during his conversion experience that has also enveloped my own thinking during my personal faith journey. Since my fallen nature is somewhat similar in certain ways to that of the self-righteous Pharisee who once said, "If others have reason for confidence in their own efforts, I have even more!" (Phil. 3:4, NLT) it is pertinent for me to examine a part of his writing that expresses his realization of a contrary truth. It is crucial to investigate a passage that delves into the heart of what Paul personally learned is essential to the message of the gospel, and that reflects his own changeover.

While traveling to a town called Damascus, Paul (who was then known as Saul) encountered the Lord Himself, in a voice and light from heaven. This glorious, powerful presence literally blinded his eyes. It appeared "as a sign that his whole life was blinded. Paul's pursuit of God was blinded. He meant well, but he was completely self-driven. It was as if God was saying, 'this is how you will walk with me: in *dependency* upon me for your thinking, acting, and teaching.'"[45] So ironically Saul's blindness made him *see* life properly.

Thus, we come upon this paradoxical principle, which lay at the center of Paul's life and ministry, which has sometimes been called Paul's personal motto (2 Cor. 12:9b): *power reaches perfection in weakness.* When the apostle acknowledged

---

45   Hans Bayer, "Life & Letters of Paul," class lecture, Covenant Theological Seminary, St. Louis, Summer 2006.

his weakness and reliance upon God, he became instantly powerful with Christ's resurrection strength.

That gets to my personal point: if Paul's realization is true, that Christ's power reaches perfection in our acknowledged personal weakness, then it rings true with something that I recently learned in a seminary class.[46] My professor explained that our gracious Lord sometimes permits affliction or suffering to free Christians from self-reliance, and to lead us to rely on God, and to more fully trust in Him. Paul describes this concept to the people of Corinth in the passionate start of his second letter to them:

> We do not want you to be uninformed, brothers, about the hardships we suffered in the province of Asia. We were under great pressure, far beyond our ability to endure, so that we despaired even of life. Indeed, in our hearts we felt the sentence of death. But this happened that we might not rely on ourselves but on God, who raises the dead.
>
> 2 Corinthians 1:8-9 (NIV)

God wanted His renewed witness to abandon his reliance upon himself. Only with complete dependence upon God could Paul be God's missionary. For that to happen, a death actually did happen within Paul. "He experienced an emotional death, and thereafter committed himself totally to God. He trusted that God was able to raise him from the dead."[47]

Previously, Paul also endured great personal suffering. Paul's aforementioned Damascus Road blinding conversion humbled him significantly. I should point out that in Acts

---

46   Hans Bayer, "Acts & Paul," class lecture, Covenant Theological Seminary, St. Louis, 27 March 2008.
47   Ibid.

9:25, we're told that, "his followers took him by night and lowered him in a basket through an opening in the wall," to save him from his plotting killers. The Lord was training Saul/Paul to depend on Him alone already!

"Conversion of Saul"

"Less is more."[49]

No one truly knows when Saul's name changed to Paul, but the first reference in the sacred record to this name change occurs while Paul was ministering on the Isle of Cyprus during his first missionary journey (Acts 13:1-9). So the change

---

48   *Conversion of Saul,* by Gustave Dore' (public domain).

49   This is a 19th century proverbial phrase, of unknown origin, often associated with the architect and furniture designer Ludwig Mies Van Der Rohe (1886-1969), a founder of modern architecture and a proponent of simplicity of style.

probably occurred by Saul's initiative, perhaps with the Lord's instruction, around Saul's conversion. Scripture does not tell us Christ's involvement in this process, but herein lies something relevant to this chapter's main point.

From his youth onward, Saul had the privilege of being trained in the most prominent rabbinical schools of that day. Among his teachers, young Saul had the honor to be trained by Gamaliel, the most outstanding and reputable rabbi teacher of that time (Acts 22:3). Gamaliel was the grandson of Hillel, the founder of the most influential rabbinical school of Judaism. Gamaliel also presided over the Sanhedrin in succession of his father. Saul's name {sow'-los} meant "desired."

Paul {pow'-los}, however, means "little" or "small." Perhaps the freshly shaken, newly changed apostle wanted to give immediate life application to this divine truth by *shrinking* with a lesser name, remembering his Lord's words:

> For he who is least among you all—he is the greatest."
> Luke 9:48 (NIV)

> Therefore, whoever humbles himself like this child is the greatest in the kingdom of heaven.
> Matthew 18:4 (NIV)

Saul was glad to be *big* and have "confidence in the flesh" (Phil. 3:4), all the way up to Damascus, but he would later tell the Philippians that it was all "rubbish (literally "dung" or "excrement"), compared to the surpassing greatness of knowing Christ Jesus my Lord." (Phil. 3:8) With a transformed attitude, *Paul* now embraced weakness, forced to realize that he was in the mighty hands of a saving God.

| MILE |

"Dear friends, I am the little servant of
an illustrious master."
-Hudson Taylor

In the beginning of this chapter, I mentioned that I had some similarities to the apostle Paul. Specifically, I've realized that my fallen nature holds on to certain Pharisaical tendencies and ways of thinking. I endured a life-changing form of physical and emotional suffering that perhaps yielded as much of a catastrophic realization as Saul's Damascus Road conversion experience, in which I also ran into an active, present God, who I found to be completely trustworthy, and worthy of my total reliance. Although I wasn't an enemy of God before this incident, our Lord brought me into a more intimate relationship with Himself, in which I would regularly learn to acknowledge my weakness, and depend on Him for strength.

I was largely unaware of my false, legalistic thinking, but in 2002, when my physical life almost *ended*, a healthier spiritual life *began* anew. Certainly today I still struggle with some legalistic tendencies, just less often, thankfully. When they do creep in, I remember that in the breath right before he stated "power is made perfect in weakness," Paul, the former "Hebrew of Hebrews" (Phil. 3:5), acknowledged his realization that God's "grace is sufficient"...

But he said to me, "My grace is sufficient for you, for my power is made perfect in weakness." Therefore I will boast all the more gladly of my weaknesses, so that the power of Christ may rest upon me. For the sake of Christ, then, I am content with weaknesses, insults, hardships, persecutions, and calamities. For when I am weak, then I am strong.

2 Corinthians 12:9-10 (ESV)

They are weak, but He is strong.
—"Jesus Loves Me"[50]

In a modern sense, as I walk out my union with Christ, especially based on what I've learned from my accident and recovery, and from Paul's conversion experience and writings, I am reminded of "Team Hoyt," the amazing Father/Son team who together have completed over 200 Triathlons. Rick is a picture of weakness, having contracted cerebral palsy at birth, but his father, Dick, is a picture of strength and power. Together, they compete. Dick swims, bikes, and runs, while pulling Rick along on a raft or cart in front or behind each time to successfully complete the Ironman Triathlons.

From a biblical narrative, this principle appears in the person of Mephibosheth (2 Samuel 9), Jonathan's crippled son, who was dependent upon the benevolence of others, specifically the grace and might of a king. Mephibosheth never recovered from his crippled condition. In the same way, we will always have our fallen natures, our (spiritually) crippled conditions on this side of glory and we, in our weakened state, are fully reliant upon a mighty and gracious king who is forever faithful, trustworthy, and true, and who is indeed, "an ever-present help in trouble" (Psalm 46:1b, NIV). In Sunday school classes,

---

50 Warner, Anna B. (w); Bradbury, William B. (m), *Jesus Loves Me* (Philadelphia, PA: J.B. Lippincott & Co., 1860).

no one ever says, "Be like Mephibosheth!" He accomplished nothing; he simply received well. And that's the key. He had no blocks, no masks, and no hindrances; his weakness and neediness were obvious and clear. Likewise, Rick Hoyt has cerebral palsy, and he always rides along in a raft or a cart while his strong dad totes him along in Ironman Triathlons.

As I consider these realities, my thoughts instantly turn to a song by my favorite contemporary Christian music artist, a man who ironically died prematurely in an automobile accident in September, 1997, at the young age of 41. Rich Mullins wrote and recorded a little-known song called "None Are Stronger," that was released six years after his death. It focuses on humility, and in each verse states, "None are stronger than the humble, and few are weaker than the proud."[51]

To give a feel for why Rich would compose such lyrics centered on humility (and an accurate biblical stance [Luke 14:11, James 4:6]), I should explain something about this humble man. Rich hated the limelight. His typical concert

"Team Hoyt"
Dick and son Rick Hoyt

uniform was jeans (with holes in the knees) and a t-shirt. No shoes. No socks. In fact, he was known for sneaking onto the stage before being introduced, because the glowing introductions always made him uncomfortable. The audience often thought the guy walking out

---

51   Rich Mullins, *None Are Stronger—Here in America* (Franklin, TN: Reunion Records, 2003), CD.

onto the dark stage and sitting at the piano was some sort of pre-concert piano tuner. He made lots of money but never saw it, because he arranged for his church to simply pay him an average American working man's salary, and give the rest to the needy. Not only that, Rich was a 36-year-old college student when his career was taking off, playing French horn in the university band.

He spoke of grace as often as possible, and I tend to think that perhaps this humble man truly understood the profound truth (that I mentioned earlier) that the Apostle Paul described in his epistle to the Corinthians, when he plainly relayed the Lord's message: "My grace is sufficient for you, for my power is made perfect in weakness" (2 Cor. 12:9, NIV). It's fair to say that Rich Mullins, like the Apostle Paul, learned to celebrate weaknesses, trials, and the things which force reliance upon a trustworthy, powerful, and gracious God, which is truly where God's power is perfected, and where we receive His all-sufficient grace.

I know that my nature tends to be "braggy," as Abby says, but whenever I start to pat myself on the back for what I think is a noteworthy accomplishment, it seems that the Lord graciously checks my spirit and says, "Remember son, you were 30 years old and wearing a diaper." Thankfully, I'm then quickly reminded that, "none are stronger than the humble, and few are weaker than the proud."[52]

> ### MILE
>
> **"Satan trembles when he sees the weakest**
> **saint upon his knees."**
> **—William Cowper**

---

52   Ibid.

When God Suffered

53

"One of the most powerful insights Christianity has bestowed to the world is that, in His tender mercy, God entered into human suffering and breathed into it the fragrance of divinity. God has been there before us."
—Alister McGrath [54]

"God does not give explanations; He gives us a Son... A Son is better than explanations."
—Austin Farrer [55]

---

53   *Nailing Christ to the Cross*, by Gustave Dore' (public domain).
54   McGrath, Alister. *The Mystery of the Cross*, Grand Rapids: Zondervan Publishing House, 1988, p. 118.
55   Austin Farrer, *A Faith of Our Own* (Cleveland: World, 1960), 34.

"Where is the God of justice?"[56] This question appeared a few thousand years ago in the days of Malachi, the prophet, and since, as the wise man indicated, "There is nothing new under the sun" (Ecc. 1:9, NIV), people like me today often wonder how an omniscient, omnipresent, benevolent God could possibly allow suffering and evil in our world, and especially in our personal, daily lives. In other words, "Why isn't God fair?"

This question was addressed once and for all 2000 years ago by Jesus, the God-man, when He suffered the worst injustice in all of history. God became a person and didn't enjoy wealth, privileges, or possessions (2 Cor. 8:9). He then endured the torment of torture and death when he was falsely accused and nailed to a cross. Indeed, He was an innocent "man of sorrows, familiar with suffering" (Isaiah 53:3, NIV). What seems most unfair of all is that Scripture states that "it was the LORD's will to crush him and cause him to suffer" (Is. 53:10, NIV), to pay for human sin and to make salvation possible, a task that Christ willingly took on, "for the joy set before Him" (Heb. 12:2, NIV). Clearly, God did not exempt himself from suffering. Rather, He feels our pain and *empathizes* with us.

Initially, Roman soldiers severely beat and tormented Him. They also plucked his beard and pierced His scalp with a crown of thorns. After the flogging, they killed Him like a common criminal in grotesque, horrific manner. These executioners, whom God Himself created (John 1:1-2), spit on Him, beat Him, nailed Him to a piece of wood, speared him, and lifted Him up for all to see.

Our Lord's incarnation is central to all of Scripture, foretold long before "the Word became flesh and blood and moved into the neighborhood" (John 1:14, The Message).

---

56   Malachi 2:17.

From the onset, the Son of God, Jesus of Nazareth, seemed to know that the pain and suffering of death was in His future, as He would say things like, "I am the good shepherd... and I lay down my life for the sheep" (John 10:14-15, NIV). No one can accuse God of not hurting as humans do, or of not understanding their physical and emotional pain. No one can accuse the Almighty of hiding Himself or of not caring. We must put to rest the idea that life must be fair, or that God is unfair. Yes, some of God's heroes in the Old Testament did suffer, but in the New Testament it was God Himself who put on skin to suffer the supreme injustice.

"My God, my God, why have you forsaken me?"
—Jesus Christ[57]

Jesus' suffering and death revealed a fallen world of horrible injustice. But the cross also made it clear that God Himself voluntarily endured such unfairness, as driven by His love for us. *Jesus was not exempt from the pain of suffering.* While freeing us from the grip of sin, God in Jesus came to share in mankind's sufferings, unjustly and unfairly.

In addition to our Lord giving us Immanuel (Isaiah 7:17, Matthew 1:23), "God with us," in the most meaningful of ways, Christ accomplished something through His suffering and death that could not have been realized in any other way, since Old Testament Law stated that "without the shedding

---

57   Matt. 27:46, Mark 15:34 (NIV).

of blood," there could be "no forgiveness of sins" (Lev. 17:11, Heb. 9:22, ESV): He established redemption for all of mankind through His suffering, an effect that even the devil did not realize (1 Cor. 2:7-9).[58]

C.S. Lewis described this same profound truth in a most simple way in his Narnia tales for children, representing Christ and Satan as Aslan and "The White Witch" respectively. In his allegory of the gospel, The Lion, the Witch and the Wardrobe, this White Witch does not understand the "deeper magic from before the dawn of time," that resulted from Aslan's sacrificial death. At one point, Aslan explains to Lucy and Susan,

> "It means that though the Witch knew the Deep Magic, there is a magic deeper still which she did not know. Her knowledge goes back only to the dawn of time. But if she could have looked a little further back, into the stillness and the darkness before Time dawned, she would have read there a different incantation. She would have known that when a willing victim who had committed no treachery was killed in a traitor's stead, the Table would crack, and Death itself would start working backward..."[59]

The "deep magic" is analogous to the God's Law, but this "deeper magic" represents the self-sacrificing, compassionate, redemptive work of Jesus Christ, His amazing *grace* which made everlasting life available to everyone.

Throughout Scripture, God has always been "compassionate and gracious" and "abounding in love."[60] So it is not surprising that, when He first gave Moses His most personal name, Yahweh (Exodus 3:14), the Lord told Moses,

---

58 Jerram Barrs, *Suffering & Evil* (St. Louis, MO: Covenant Theological Seminary, 2002), CD.

59 C.S. Lewis, The Lion the Witch and the Wardrobe (New York. NY: HarperCollins, 1978), Ch. 15.

60 Exodus 34:6, Neh. 9:17, Psalm 86:15, 103:8, Joel 2:13, Jonah 4:2.

"I have indeed seen the misery of my people in Egypt... and I am concerned about their suffering." (Exodus 3:7, NIV) Moreover, it is not shocking that when God became flesh, He lived to suffer and die, out of His love for us. Finally, it is not unexpected that today, He still promises to be with us always (Mt. 28:20), even when we have to endure the worst forms of trials and sufferings. He is, indeed, an "ever-present help in trouble." (Psalm 46:1, NIV)

"The Son of Man will be handed over to sinners who will nail him to a cross. But three days later he will rise to life."
Luke 24:7 (CEV)

EPILOGUE

A Gracious Scar

Scar—n. a mark left after a wound has healed[61]

**"You can look at a scar and see hurt,
or you can look at a scar and see healing."
—Sheri Reynolds[62]**

B y medical definition, "When a wound heals, a *scar* takes its place."[63] So a scar is not a mark of *hurting*, but of *healing*. Therefore, as you've read the pages of this book, please know upfront that my faith, while shaken in 2002, still stands in a living God who is committed to healing,

---

61   American Heritage Dictionary
62   *A Gracious Plenty,* referring to Finch Nobles, a fortyish woman burned as a child and scarred for life, p. 80.
63   www.emedicine.com

restoration, and our welfare, but, at the same time, who is certainly a God of mystery who leaves us with our fair share of unanswered questions. The reason that I carefully define "scar" is that this book's central focus is on a fatality and a horrible set of injuries, and the after effects in the weeks, months, and years that follow. And life on this side of glory is certainly full of hurts.

I have either stated or implied what roles I believe are divine, but I am in no way insinuating that God *did* any of the wounding or damaging, physically or emotionally. Rather, He was the One who initiated multiple processes of healing and restoration. You've read about such initiatives in this book, and how I now trust more than ever that God is, "an ever-present help in trouble." (Psalm 46:1), and how I can testify to the truth of His ongoing amazing *grace*.

When I see the scar on my forehead in the mirror each morning, I'm reminded of the Biblical account of Jacob's wrestling match with God (Genesis 32:24-32), since it seems that Jacob lived the rest of his days with a limp (Genesis 32:31, Heb. 11:21), *a limp that was a daily reminder of God's personal gracious blessings* to him, and of his face-to-face interaction with God Himself[64]. My scar is somewhat similar to Jacob's limp, in that I too have a daily reminder of God's grace, blessings, and presence. In other words, it's fair to say that I am "scarred by grace."

> **MILE**

"There but by the grace of God go I." [65]
—John Bradford, 1510-1555

---

64 The name of the place where Jacob wrestled with the Lord is "Peniel," which means, "face of God."

65 Attributed to John Bradford, English Reformer, while in prison for his faith observing a criminal on his way to be executed for his crimes.

Thro' many dangers, toils and snares,
I have already come;
'Tis grace has brought me safe thus far,
And grace will lead me home.[66]

---

66   Words: John Newton, Music: Olney Hymns, London: W. Oliver, *Amazing Grace,* 3rd stanza (1779).

APPENDIX

Abby's Song

Abby actually wrote the words to this song 3 years ago while in Texas with her grandparents (Jill's parents). "Papa Jakie" wrote the music and plays it on piano while Abby sings it.

"Oh Lord, I Love You"
Words by Abby Mirikitani, age 7

Oh, how great and good you are, Lord.
Your power turns it all around.
You, Lord, have love inside of You.
Oh Lord, I love You!

My Delight

Illustrated by Emily Lambert

*For our 4th Anniversary, I took this song that I'd
written Christe a few years before, and asked our
sweet artist friend, Emily, if she could create a
children's book out of it for me to give to Christe, so she
could read it to Josiah at his bedtime.
JoJo LOVES it!!!*

Once a man (that's Daddy) had a delight,
And though she was quite small, (that's Abby)
To him she was so sweet and dear
That to her he gave his all.

So in her little heart & soul
He focused all his time,
And loving, faithful Immanuel (that's our God)
Equipped his one-tracked mind.

But then one day God
turned his eyes
To see a pretty treat (that's Mommy)
They met, they talked,
and soon he saw
This one was also sweet!

And she was smart too,
    he learned,
She was exactly right.
Before he knew it, the man
    had found
A completely new delight. (that's Mommy)

When You Need Help, Don't Hesitate. Call 9-1-1!

By Gregg Bettis

This story comes courtesy of my friend, Gregg Bettis. As President of Kids Across America Kamps, he holds a front row seat to dramatic transformation stories. Seldom have I met anyone with as much enthusiasm and tireless energy in relentlessly pursuing their call. Gregg would tell you it's his privilege. This time, the story just happened to be his:

At 6 pm on June 10th, 2004 on a "routine" final approach into a small private airpark on the beautiful shores of Table Rock Lake, in Southwest Missouri, suddenly without warning, a powerful right quartering wind shear slammed into the rear of my small high performance airplane forcing me sharply off course to the left.

Almost immediately after applying full power for a go around and pushing full right rudder, my left wing tip struck the top of an 80' tree near the edge of the runway at 120 mph. I literally watched my propeller fold up like a paper clip as I crashed through the top branches of another nearby tree and then dive full speed into the ground.

The last thing I distinctly remember before the impact of the crash and waking up in the hospital was being in perfect peace. In a flash, the Holy Spirit brought to mind Psalm 91:1 ("He who calls out to the Most High, shall abide under the shadow of the Almighty")...and I rapidly cried out to God three times, "Oh God help me, Oh God help me, Oh God help me."

With puddles in my eyes, I share my story with you because I am absolutely convinced that the power of heaven is unlocked on earth when we give ourselves to the intimacy of abiding in the very presence of the Almighty. God heard and answered my call and He is obviously not finished with me or with you yet.

My earnest prayer for all who read or hears my story, for all of my friends and family and for every precious young person who comes through our gates at Kids Across America Kamps is that you and they might gain a renewed momentum. I hope you experience a holy fascination to pursue the greatest pearl of human existence...a personal, intimate, passionate, living relationship with the glorious Creator of the universe.

Perhaps, you or someone you know will need help. If so, call 9-1-1...Psalm 91:1 and I can assure you that He will hear you, and He will answer you. In addition, like me, you too will no doubt experience new dimensions of His kingdom power and glory!

Streams in the Desert

These are very meaningful and relevant devotionals that I came across in <u>Streams in the Desert</u> that I think will bless you too.

<u>Reaching Perfection</u>   <u>Tuesday, July 13, 2010</u>

"Perfect through suffering" (Heb. 2:10).

Steel is iron plus fire. Soil is rock, plus heat, or glacier crushing. Linen is flax plus the bath that cleans, the comb that separates, and the flail that pounds, and the shuttle that weaves. Human character must have a plus attached to it. The world does not forget great characters. But great characters are not made of luxuries, they are made by suffering.

I heard of a mother who brought into her home as a companion to her own son, a crippled boy who was also a hunchback. She had warned her boy to be very careful in his relations to him, and not to touch the sensitive part of his life but go right on playing with him as if he were an ordinary boy. She listened to her son as they were playing; and after a few minutes he said to his companion: "Do you know what you have got on your back?" The little hunchback was embarrassed, and he hesitated a moment. The boy said: "It is the box in which your wings are; and some day God is going to cut it open, and then you will fly away and be an angel."

Some day, God is going to reveal the fact to every Christian, that the very principles they now rebel against, have been the instruments which He used in perfecting their characters and moulding them into perfection, polished stones for His great building yonder.—Cortland Myers

Suffering is a wonderful fertilizer to the roots of character. The great object of this life is character. This is the only thing we can carry with us into eternity... To gain the most of it and the best of it is the object of probation.—Austin Phelps

"By the thorn road and no other is the mount of vision won."

Free Through Suffering   Friday, October 1, 2010

"Thou hast enlarged me when I was in distress" (Ps. 4:1).

This is one of the grandest testimonies ever given by man to the moral government of God. It is not a man's thanksgiving that he has been set free from suffering. It is a thanksgiving that he has been set free through suffering: "Thou hast enlarged me when I was in distress." He declares the sorrows of life to have been themselves the source of life's enlargement.

And have not you and I a thousand times felt this to be true? It is written of Joseph in the dungeon that "the iron entered into his soul." We all feel that what Joseph needed for his soul was just the iron. He had seen only the glitter of the gold. He had been rejoicing in youthful dreams; and dreaming hardens the heart. He who sheds tears over a romance will not be most apt to help reality; real sorrow will be too unpoetic for him. We need the iron to enlarge our nature. The gold is but a vision; the iron is an experience. The chain which unites me to humanity must be an iron chain. That touch of nature which makes the world akin is not joy, but sorrow; gold is partial, but iron is universal.

My soul, if thou wouldst be enlarged into human sympathy, thou must be narrowed into limits of human suffering. Joseph's dungeon is the road to Joseph's throne. Thou canst not lift the iron load of thy brother if the iron hath not entered into thee. It is thy limit that is thine enlargement. It is the shadows of thy life that are the real fulfillment of thy dreams of glory. Murmur not at the shadows; they are better revelations than thy dreams. Say not that the shades of the prison-house have fettered thee; thy fetters are wings--wings of flight into the bosom of humanity. The door of thy prison-house is a door into the heart of the universe. God has enlarged thee by the binding of sorrow's chain. --George Matheson

If Joseph had not been Egypt's prisoner, he had never been Egypt's governor. The iron chain about his feet ushered in the golden chain about his neck.--Selected

---

Alone With God   Saturday, August 7, 2010

"And Jacob was left alone; and there wrestled a man with him until the breaking of the day" (Gen. 32:24).

Left alone! What different sensations those words conjure up to each of us. To some they spell loneliness and desolation, to others rest and quiet. To be left alone without God, would be too awful for words, but to be left alone with Him is a foretaste of Heaven! If His followers spent more time alone with Him, we should have spiritual giants again.

The Master set us an example. Note how often He went to be alone with God; and He had a mighty purpose behind the command, "When thou prayest, enter into thy closet, and when thou hast shut thy door, pray."

The greatest miracles of Elijah and Elisha took place when they were alone with God. It was alone with God that Jacob became a prince; and just there that we, too, may become princes—"men (aye, and women too!) wondered at" (Zech. 3:8). Joshua was alone when the Lord came to him. (Josh. 1:1) Gideon and Jephthah were by themselves when commissioned to save Israel. (Judges 6:11 and 11:29) Moses was by himself at the wilderness bush. (Exodus 3:1-5) Cornelius was praying by himself when the angel came to him. (Acts 10:2) No one was with Peter on the house top, when he was instructed to go to the Gentiles. (Acts 10:9) John the Baptist was alone in the wilderness (Luke 1:90), and John the Beloved alone in Patmos, when nearest God. (Rev. 1:9)

Covet to get alone with God. If we neglect it, we not only rob ourselves, but others too, of blessing, since when we are blessed we are able to pass on blessing to others. It may mean less outside work; it must mean more depth and power, and the consequence, too, will be "they saw no man save Jesus only."

To be alone with God in prayer cannot be over-emphasized.

"If chosen men had never been alone,
In deepest silence open-doored to God,
No greatness ever had been dreamed or done."

Joined in God   February 19

"As sorrowful, yet always rejoicing" (2 Cor. 6:10).

Sorrow was beautiful, but her beauty was the beauty of the moonlight shining through the leafy branches of the trees in the wood, and making little pools of silver here and there on the soft green moss below.

When Sorrow sang, her notes were like the low sweet call of the nightingale, and in her eyes was the unexpectant gaze of one who has ceased to look for coming gladness. She could weep in tender sympathy with those who weep, but to rejoice with those who rejoice was unknown to her.

Joy was beautiful, too, but his was the radiant beauty of the summer morning. His eyes still held the glad laughter of childhood, and his hair had the glint of the sunshine's kiss. When Joy sang his voice soared upward as the lark's, and his step was the step of a conqueror who has never known defeat. He could rejoice with all who rejoice, but to weep with those who weep was unknown to him.

"But we can never be united," said Sorrow wistfully.

"No, never." And Joy's eyes shadowed as he spoke. "My path lies through the sunlit meadows, the sweetest roses bloom for my gathering, and the blackbirds and thrushes await my coming to pour forth their most joyous lays."

"My path," said Sorrow, turning slowly away, "leads through the darkening woods, with moon-flowers only shall my hands be filled. Yet the sweetest of all earth-songs—the love song of the night—shall be mine; farewell, Joy, farewell."

Even as she spoke they became conscious of a form standing beside them; dimly seen, but of a Kingly Presence, and a great and holy awe stole over them as they sank on their knees before Him.

"I see Him as the King of Joy," whispered Sorrow, "for on His Head are many crowns, and the nailprints in His hands and feet are the scars of a great victory. Before Him all my sorrow is melting away into deathless love and gladness, and I give myself to Him forever."

"Nay, Sorrow," said Joy softly, "but I see Him as the King of Sorrow, and the crown on His head is a crown of thorns, and the nailprints in His hands and feet are the scars of a great agony. I, too, give myself to Him forever, for sorrow with Him must be sweeter than any joy that I have known."

"Then we are one in Him," they cried in gladness, "for none but He could unite Joy and Sorrow."

Hand in hand they passed out into the world to follow Him through storm and sunshine, in the bleakness of winter cold and the warmth of summer gladness, "as sorrowful yet always rejoicing."

"Should Sorrow lay her hand upon thy shoulder,
And walk with thee in silence on life's way,
While Joy, thy bright companion once, grown colder,
Becomes to thee more distant day by day?
Shrink not from the companionship of Sorrow,
She is the messenger of God to thee;
And thou wilt thank Him in His great tomorrow
For what thou knowest not now, thou then shalt see;
She is God's angel, clad in weeds of night,
With 'whom we walk by faith and not by sight.'"

Strength From the Sorrow   Thursday, August 19, 2010

"Now it came to pass after the death of Moses, the servant of the Lord, that the Lord spake unto Joshua, the son of Nun, Moses' minister, saying, Moses my servant is dead; now, therefore arise, go over this Jordan, thou and all this people" (Joshua 1:1-2).

Sorrow came to you yesterday, and emptied your home. Your first impulse now is to give up, and sit down in despair amid the wrecks of your hopes. But you dare not do it. You are in the line of battle, and the crisis is at hand. To falter a moment would be to imperil some holy interest. Other lives would be harmed by your pausing, holy interests would suffer, should your hands be folded. You must not linger even to indulge your grief.

A distinguished general related this pathetic incident of his own experience in time of war. The general's son was a lieutenant of battery. An assault was in progress. The father was leading his division in a charge; as he pressed on in the field, suddenly his eye was caught by the sight of a dead battery-officer lying just before him. One glance showed him it was his own son. His fatherly impulse was to stop beside the loved form and give vent to his grief, but the duty of the moment demanded that he should press on in the charge; so, quickly snatching one hot kiss from the dead lips, he hastened away, leading his command in the assault.

Weeping inconsolably beside a grave can never give back love's banished treasure, nor can any blessing come out of such sadness. Sorrow makes deep scars; it writes its record ineffaceably on the heart which suffers. We really never get over our great griefs; we are never altogether the same after we have passed through them as we were before. Yet there is a humanizing and fertilizing influence in sorrow which has been rightly accepted and cheerfully borne. Indeed, they are poor who have never suffered, and have none of sorrow's marks upon them. The joy set before us should shine upon our grief as the sun shines through the clouds, glorifying them. God has so ordered, that in pressing on in duty we shall find the truest, richest comfort for ourselves. Sitting down to brood over our sorrows, the darkness deepens about us and creeps into our heart, and our strength changes to weakness. But, if we turn away from the gloom, and take up the tasks and duties to which God calls us, the light will come again, and we shall grow stronger.—J. R. Miller

Thou knowest that through our tears Of hasty, selfish
weeping
Comes surer sin, and for our petty fears of loss thou hast
in keeping
A greater gain than all of which we dreamed; Thou knowest
that in grasping
The bright possessions which so precious seemed we lose
them; but if, clasping
Thy faithful hand, we tread with steadfast feet the path of
thy appointing,
There waits for us a treasury of sweet delight, royal
anointing
With oil of gladness and of strength.

—Helen Hunt Jackson

It Is Sufficient   February 6

"IS" (2 Cor. 12:9).

It had pleased God to remove my youngest child under circumstances of peculiar trial and pain; and as I had just laid my little one's body in the churchyard, on return home, I felt it my duty to preach to my people on the meaning of trial.

Finding that this text was in the lesson for the following Sabbath, I chose it as my Master's message to them and myself; but on trying to prepare the notes, I found that in honesty I could not say that the words were true; and therefore I knelt down and asked God to let His grace be sufficient for me. While I was thus pleading, I opened my eyes and saw a framed illuminated text, which my mother had given me only a few days before, and which I had told my servant to place upon the wall during my absence at the holiday resort where my little one was taken away from us.

I did not notice the words on returning to my house; but as I looked up and wiped my eyes, the words met my gaze, "My grace is sufficient for thee."

The "is" was picked out in bright green while the "My" and the "thee" were painted in another color.

In one moment the message came straight to my soul, as a rebuke for offering such a prayer as, "Lord, let Thy grace be sufficient for me"; for the answer was almost as an audible voice, "How dare you ask that which is?" God cannot make it any more sufficient than He has made it; get up and believe it, and you will find it true, because the Lord says it in the simplest way: "My grace is (not shall be or may be) sufficient for thee."

"My," "is," and "thee" were from that moment, I hope, indelibly fixed upon my heart; and I (thank God) have been trying to live in the reality of the message from that day forward to the present time.

The lesson that came to me, and which I seek to convey to others, is, Never turn God's facts into hopes, or prayers, but simply use them as realities, and you will find them powerful as you believe them.—Prebendary H. W. Webb Peploe

He giveth more grace when the burdens grow greater,
He sendeth more strength when the labors increase;
To added affliction He addeth His mercies,
To multiplied trials His multiplied peace.

When we have exhausted our store of endurance,
When our strength has failed ere the day is half done,
When we reach the end of our hoarded resources
Our Father's full giving is only begun.
His love has no limit, His grace has no measure,

His power no boundary known unto men;
For out of His infinite riches in Jesus
He giveth and giveth and giveth again.

—Annie Johnson Flint

Cast Your Burdens Upon God   Tuesday, August 17, 2010

"Look from the top" (Song of Solomon 4:8).

Crushing weights give the Christian wings. It seems like a contradiction in terms, but it is a blessed truth. David out of some bitter experience cried: "Oh, that I had wings like a dove! Then would I fly away, and be at rest" (Ps. 55:6). But before he finished this meditation he seems to have realized that his wish for wings was a realizable one. For he says, "Cast thy burden upon Jehovah, and he will sustain thee."

The word "burden" is translated in the Bible margin, "what he (Jehovah) hath given thee." The saints' burdens are God-given; they lead him to "wait upon Jehovah," and when that is done, in the magic of trust, the "burden" is metamorphosed into a pair of wings, and the weighted one "mounts up with wings as eagles. —Sunday School Times

One day when walking down the street,
On business bent, while thinking hard
About the "hundred cares" which seemed
Like thunder clouds about to break
In torrents, Self-pity said to me:

"You poor, poor thing, you have too much
To do. Your life is far too hard.
This heavy load will crush you soon."
A swift response of sympathy
Welled up within. The burning sun
Seemed more intense. The dust and noise
Of puffing motors flying past
With rasping blast of blowing horn
Incensed still more the whining nerves,
The fabled last back-breaking straw
To weary, troubled, fretting mind.

"Ah, yes, 'twill break and crush my life;
I cannot bear this constant strain
Of endless, aggravating cares;

They are too great for such as I."
So thus my heart condoled itself,
"Enjoying misery," when lo!
A "still small voice" distinctly said,
"Twas sent to lift you—not to crush."

I saw at once my great mistake.
My place was not beneath the load
But on the top! God meant it not
That I should carry it. He sent
It here to carry me. Full well
He knew my incapacity
Before the plan was made. He saw
A child of His in need of grace
And power to serve; a puny twig
Requiring sun and rain to grow;
An undeveloped chrysalis;
A weak soul lacking faith in God.

He could not help but see all this
And more. And then, with tender thought
He placed it where it had to grow—
Or die. To lie and cringe beneath
One's load means death, but life and power
Await all those who dare to rise above.
Our burdens are our wings; on them
We soar to higher realms of grace;
Without them we must roam for aye
On planes of undeveloped faith,
(For faith grows but by exercise in circumstance
impossible).

Oh, paradox of Heaven. The load We think will crush was sent to lift us Up to God! Then, soul of mine, Climb up! for naught can e'er be crushed Save what is underneath the weight. How may we climb! By what ascent Shall we surmount the carping cares Of life! Within His word is found The key which opes His secret stairs; Alone with Christ, secluded there, We mount our loads, and rest in Him.—Miss Mary Butterfield

---

Run With Patience
"Let us run with patience" (Heb. 12:1)

O run with patience is a very difficult thing. Running is apt to suggest the absence of patience, the eagerness to reach the goal. We commonly associate patience with lying down. We think of it as the angel that guards the couch of the invalid. Yet, I do not think the invalid's patience the hardest to achieve.

There is a patience which I believe to be harder—the patience that can run. To lie down in the time of grief, to be quiet under the stroke of adverse fortune, implies a great strength; but I know of something that implies a strength greater still: It is the power to work under a stroke; to have a great weight at your heart and still to run; to have a deep anguish in your spirit and still perform the daily task. It is a Christlike thing!

Many of us would nurse our grief without crying if we were allowed to nurse it. The hard thing is that most of us are called to exercise our patience, not in bed, but in the street. We are called to bury our sorrows, not in lethargic quiescence, but in active service—in the exchange, in the workshop, in the hour of social intercourse, in the contribution to another's joy. There is no burial of sorrow so difficult as that; it is the "running with patience."

This was Thy patience, O Son of man! It was at once a waiting and a running—a waiting for the goal, and a doing of the lesser work meantime. I see Thee at Cana turning the water into wine lest the marriage feast should be clouded. I see Thee in the desert feeding a multitude with bread just to relieve a temporary want. All, all the time, Thou wert bearing a mighty grief, unshared, unspoken. Men ask for a rainbow in the cloud; but I would ask more from Thee. I would be, in my cloud, myself a rainbow—a minister to others' joy. My patience will be perfect when it can work in the vineyard.—George Matheson

> "When all our hopes are gone,
> 'Tis well our hands must keep toiling on
> For others' sake:
> For strength to bear is found in duty done;
> And he is best indeed who learns to make
> The joy of others cure his own heartache."